KU-592-582

The Yoga COOK BOOK

Vegetarian Food for Body and Mind

Recipes from the Sivananda Yoga Vedanta Centres

GAIA
GAIA BOOKS

A GAIA ORIGINAL

Books from Gaia celebrate the vision of Gaia,
the self-sustaining living Earth, and seek to help its
readers live in greater personal and planetary harmony.

Editor	*Felicity Jackson*
Designer	*Sara Mathews*
Photographer	*Adrian Swift*
Home economist	*Carol Tennant*
Managing Editor	*Pip Morgan*
Project co-ordinator for Sivananda Yoga Vedanta Centres	*Swami Saradananda*
Direction	*Patrick Nugent*

Publisher's Note

This publication contains the opinions and ideas of the Sivananda Yoga
Vedanta centres and is designed to provide useful advice to the reader on
the subject matter covered. The publisher and author specifically disclaim
any responsibility for any liability, loss or risk which may be claimed or
incurred as a consequence, directly or indirectly, of the use of any of the
contents of this publication

® This is a Registered Trade Mark of Gaia Books
an imprint of Octopus Publishing Group
2–4 Heron Quays, London E14 4JP

Copyright © 2005 Gaia Books
Text Copyright © 1998, 2005 by The Sivananda Yoga
Centre

The right of Sivananda Yoga Centres to be identified as the
author of this work has been asserted in accordance with
Sections 77 and 78 of the Copyright, Designs and Patents
Act 1988, United Kingdom.

All rights reserved including the right of
reproduction in whole or in part in any form.

First published in the United Kingdom in 1999 by Gaia
Books Ltd

ISBN 1-85675-245-3
EAN 9 781856 752459

A catalogue record of this book is available
from the British Library.

Printed in China

10 9 8 7 6 5 4 3 2 1

Acknowledgements
Gaia Books would like to thank:
*Home economists: Anne Sheasby, Angela Bogginao and
Steven Wheeler and all those who tested the recipes;
assistant to Carol Tennant: Kate Jay; models: Naya and
Tejas; design assistants: Phil Gamble and Matt Moate;
Crown Publishers for permission to reproduce quotes
from* The Complete Illustrated Book of Yoga *by Swami
Vishnu-devananda copyright © 1960, 1988 by the Julian
Press, Inc.*

CONTENTS

The Sivananda Yoga Centres would like to thank:
Shakti Warwick (New York) for inspiring, writing and compiling recipes for the first draft of this book; Shanti Smith (London) for doing the second draft and for developing the recipes into a publishable form; Uma Miller (Quebec) for compiling the 'Sivananda Cookbook' from which many of the recipes were taken; Prema Venugopalan for the South Indian Bandara spread; Nigel Walker, Swami Radhapriyananda, Swami Gayatrianananda, Ganesha, Kamala, Prema and Dattatreya, and so many others for contributing recipes; Jaya and Padmavati for organising, Poorna and her team of dedicated Karma Yogis for testing, and all the students of the London Sivananda Yoga Centre for their patience in allowing the recipes to be tested on them.

The Sivananda Yoga Vedanta Centres are a worldwide network of teaching facilities with international headquarters in Val Morin, Quebec, Canada. Founded by Swami Vishnu-devananda, recognized as one of the foremost authorities on Hatha and Raja Yoga, the purpose of the centres is to promote the teaching of the ancient science of yoga.

A native of South India, Swamiji (as he was popularly known) arrived in the West in 1957, after being sent by his teacher, Swami Sivananda, with the words "people are waiting." Dedicating his life to the cause of peace, both as inner discipline and on a global level, Swamiji realized that today, more than any other time in history, people are facing daily stresses and tensions that are beyond their control. He had a vision of how the age-old techniques of yoga could be used to solve many of the pressing problems of modern life, such as ill health, stress, personal alienation and even war.

Swamiji synthesized the ancient wisdom of yoga into five principles, upon which he based his *The Complete Illustrated Book of Yoga*. Several years later he followed with *Meditation and Mantras*, one of the most complete sourcebooks available. He wrote a commentary on the ancient scripture, *Hatha Yoga Pradipika* and was the inspiration behind both *The Book of Yoga* and *Yoga Mind & Body*.

Swami Vishnu-devananda left his body in November 1993. Now there are 25 Sivananda Yoga Vedanta Centres and Ashrams, with many other affiliated centres and teachers, around the world.

Ashram Addresses

Sivananda Ashram Yoga Camp
673, 8th Avenue
Val Morin
Quebec J0T 2R0
CANADA
Tel: +1.819.322.3226
Fax: +1.819.322.5876
e-mail: HQ@sivananda.org

Sivananda Ashram Yoga Ranch
P.O. Box 195, Budd Road
Woodbourne, NY 12788
U.S.A.
Tel: +1.845.436.6492
Fax: +1.845.434.1032
e-mail: YogaRanch@sivananda.org

Sivananda Ashram Yoga Retreat
P.O. Box N7550
Paradise Island, Nassau
BAHAMAS
Tel: +1.242.363.2902
Fax: +1.242.363.3783
e-mail: Nassau@sivananda.org

Sivananda Yoga Vedanta
Dhanwantari Ashram
P.O.Neyyar Dam
Thiruvananthapuram Dt.
Kerala, 695 572
INDIA
Tel: +91.471.2273.093
Fax: +91.471.2272.093
e-mail: YogaIndia@sivananda.org

Sivananda Ashram Yoga Farm
14651 Ballantree Lane, Comp. 8
Grass Valley, CA 95949
U.S.A.
Tel: +1.530.272.9322
Fax: +1.530.477.6054
USA: 1-800-469-9642
e-mail: YogaFarm@sivananda.org

Sivananda Yoga Vedanta
Meenakshi Ashram
Kalloothu, Saramthangi Village
Vellayampatti P.O., Palamedu (via)
Vadippatti Taluk, Madurai Dist.
625 503 Tamil Nadu
INDIA
Tel: +91.452. 209.0662
e-mail: madurai@sivananda.org

Sivananda Kutir
P.O. Netala, Uttara Kashi Dt
(near Siror Bridge)
Uttaranchal, Himalayas, 249 193
INDIA
Tel: +91.1374.222624/236296
Fax: +91.1374.224159
e-mail: himalayas@sivananda.org

Sivananda Yoga Retreat House
Am Bichlachweg 40A
A- 6370 Reith bei Kitzbuhel
AUSTRIA
Tel: +43.5356.67.404
Fax: +43.5356.67.4044
e-mail: tyrol@sivananda.net

Chateau du Yoga Sivananda
26 Impasse du Bignon
45170 Neuville aux bois
FRANCE
Tel: +33.2.38.91.88.82
Fax: +33.2.38.91.18.09
e-mail: orleans@sivananda.net

CENTRE ADDRESSES

ARGENTINA
Centro Internacional de Yoga
Sivananda
Julian Alvarez 2201
CP 1425 Buenos Aires
ARGENTINA
Tel: +54.11.4827.9269 /9566
Fax: +54.11.4827.9512
e-mail:
BuenosAires@sivananda.org

AUSTRIA
Sivananda Yoga Vedanta Zentrum
Prinz-Eugenstrasse 18
A-1040 Vienna, AUSTRIA
Tel:: +43.1.586.3453
Fax: +43.1.587.1551
e-mail: Vienna@sivananda.net

CANADA
Sivananda Yoga Vedanta Centre
5178 St Lawrence Blvd
Montreal, Quebec H2T 1R8,
CANADA
Tel: +1.514.279.3545
Fax: +1.514.279.3527
e-mail: Montreal@sivananda.org

Sivananda Yoga Vedanta Centre
77 Harbord Street
Toronto, Ontario M5S 1G4,
CANADA
Tel: +1.416.966.9642
e-mail: Toronto@sivananda.org

FRANCE
Centre Sivananda de Yoga
Vedanta
123 Boulevard de Sebastopol
F-75002 Paris, FRANCE
TEL: +33.1.40.26.77.49
Tel: +33.1.42.33.51.97
e-mail: Paris@sivananda.net

GERMANY
Sivananda Yoga Vedanta Zentrum
Steinheilstrasse 1
D-80333 Munich, GERMANY
Tel: +49.89.52.44.76
Fax: +49.89.52.91.28
e-mail: Munich@sivananda.net

INDIA
Sivananda Yoga Vedanta Zentrum
Schmiljanstrasse 24
D-12161 Berlin, GERMANY
Tel: +49.30.8599.9799
Fax: +49.30.8599.9797
e-mail: Berlin@sivananda.net

Sivananda Yoga Vedanta
Nataraja Centre
A-41 Kailash Colony
New Delhi 110 048, INDIA
Tel: +91.11.2648.0869 /
2645.3962
e-mail: Delhi@sivananda.org

Sivananda Yoga Vedanta Centre
House No.18, TC 36/1238
Subhash Nagar
Vallakkadavu PO, Perunthanni,
Trivandrum,
695 008, Kerala, INDIA
Tel: +91.471.245.1398/ 245.0942
Fax: +91.471.246.5368
e-mail: Trivandrum@sivananda.org

Sivananda Yoga Vedanta Centre
3/655 (Plot No. 131) Kaveri Nagar
Kuppam Road
Kottivakkam, Chennai (Madras)
600 041
INDIA
Tel: +91.44.2451.1626/ 2451.2546
e-mail: Madras@sivananda.org

Sivananda Yoga Vedanta Centre
Plot # 23, Dr Sathar Road
Anna Nagar, Madurai 625 025
Tamil Nadu, INDIA
Tel: +91.452.252.1170
Fax: +91.452.539.3445
e-mail: maduraicentre@sivanan-
da.org

ISRAEL
Sivananda Yoga Vedanta Centre
6 Lateris St., Tel Aviv 64166,
ISRAEL
Tel: +972.3.691.6793
Fax: +972.3.696.3939
e-mail: TelAviv@sivananda.org

SPAIN
Centro de Yoga Sivananda
Vedanta
Calle Eraso 4
E-28028 Madrid, SPAIN
Tel: +34.91.361.5150
Fax: +34.91.361.5194
e-mail: Madrid@sivananda.net

SWITZERLAND
Centre Sivananda de Yoga
Vedanta
1 Rue des Minoteries
CH-1205 Geneva, SWITZERLAND
Tel: +41.22.328.03.28
Fax: +41.22.328.03.59
e-mail: Geneva@sivananda.net

URUGUAY
Asociacion de Yoga Sivananda
Acevedo Diaz 1523
11200 Montevideo, URUGUAY
Tel: +598.2.401.09.29 / 401.66.85
Fax: +598.2.400.73.88
e-mail: Montevideo@sivananda.org

UNITED KINGDOM
Sivananda Yoga Vedanta Centre
51 Felsham Road
London SW15 1AZ
UNITED KINGDOM
Tel: +44.20.8780.0160
Fax: +44.20.8780.0128
e-mail: London@sivananda.net

UNITED STATES
Sivananda Yoga Vedanta Center
1246 Bryn Mawr
Chicago, IL 60660, USA
Tel: +1.773.878.7771
Fax: +1.773.878.7527
e-mail: Chicago@sivananda.org

Sivananda Yoga Vedanta Centre
243 West 24th Street
New York, NY 10011, USA
Tel: +1.212.255.4560
Fax: +1.212.727.7392
e-mail: NewYork@sivananda.org

Sivananda Yoga Vedanta Center
1200 Arguello Blvd
San Francisco, CA 94122, USA
Tel: +1.415.681.2731
Fax: +1.415.681.5162
e-mail:
SanFrancisco@sivananda.org

Sivananda Yoga Vedanta Center
13325 Beach Avenue
Marina del Rey, CA 90292, USA
Tel: +1.310.822.9642
e-mail: LosAngeles@sivananda.org

INTRODUCTION

Yogis believe that
"the expression of the spirit increases in proportion to the
development of the body and mind in which it is encased.
Therefore, yoga prescribes methods to train and develop
the physical body and mind."

Swami Vishnu-devananda,
The Complete Illustrated Book of Yoga

The physical body is seen as an instrument, or vehicle, for the soul on its journey towards perfection. Just like other vehicles, this body/car has specific requirements which must be fulfilled for it to function smoothly and supply the optimum mileage. These requirements are the five yogic principles: proper exercise; proper breathing; proper relaxation; proper diet; and positive thinking and meditation.

Proper exercise acts as a lubricating routine. In yoga, physical exercises called asanas (the Sanskrit word means 'steady pose') help to keep the joints, muscles and other parts of the body functioning properly by increasing circulation and flexibility.

Proper breathing aids the body in connecting to its battery, the Solar Plexus, where tremendous potential energy is stored. When tapped through specific yoga breathing techniques, known as pranayama, this energy is released for physical and mental rejuvenation in the body.

Proper relaxation cools down the system as does the radiator of a car. When the body and mind are continually overworked, their efficiency diminishes. Relaxation is Nature's way of recharging the body and mind.

Proper diet provides the correct type of fuel. The body gets the energy it needs to work, grow and maintain itself from the prana (vital energy), air, water and food. The yogic diet is a vegetarian one, consisting of pure, natural foods that promote good health and optimum vitality.

Positive thinking and meditation puts you in control. Just as any vehicle requires an intelligent driver, so the body needs a balanced mind. Regular meditation helps to clear and focus your mind and improve your ability to concentrate. Positive thinking will purify the intellect and help you to begin to experience wisdom and inner peace.

The Yogic Diet

This cookbook is concerned with the basic tenets of a 'proper' yogic diet, traditionally a lacto-vegetarian one, consisting of grains, pulses, fruits, vegetables, nuts, seeds and dairy products. As well as being simple, natural and wholesome, this diet takes into account the subtle effect that food has on the mind and the prana.

The question of whether humans are meant to be vegetarians is a topic that has been discussed by everyone from philosophers to anatomists. As far as health is concerned, meat is high in cholesterol and uric acid, as well as additives and preservatives – all of which contribute to a multitude of diseases. A mainly meat diet has been found to be a major contributor to such modern problems as high blood pressure, heart attacks, hardening of the arteries, arthritis and gout. Excess uric acid lodged in the joints contributes to arthritis, while arteries clogged with cholesterol and other fatty deposits decrease the flow of blood to the brain, contributing to senility and raised blood pressure.

As if this is not bad enough, we are reminded that the meat business is run like a modern factory – cattle are seen as only so much saleable poundage. While on the hoof, animals are loaded up with mega-doses of antibiotics to prevent illness (and loss of profits). Much of the residue of these hormones and antibiotics is left in the cells of the animals and consequently goes into the consumer's system. It is also interesting to note that even the most dedicated of meat-eaters in the West would shy away from eating a carnivorous animal, such as a cat or a dog. Perhaps this aversion is natural. As all energy originates from the Sun, we instinctively realize that the closer to the source we eat, the more potent is that energy.

The many physical reasons for being a vegetarian do not need to be discussed in detail here. Let it suffice to say that animal protein is not necessary for good health: there are many other sources of protein, such as pulses, nuts and seeds, as well as better vegetable sources of carbohydrates, fats, fibre, vitamins and minerals – all of the nutrients that we strive to access in our food. Having said that, let us turn to the psychological and spiritual basis for vegetarianism.

The animal world, for the most part, is a round of slaughter – the stronger or more cunning killing the weaker in order to survive, until they are devoured by an even mightier opponent. The difference with human beings is that we are endowed with intellect and free will, and so possess the ability to side-step a portion of this cycle and live in harmony with other life forms rather than in contest with them. The law of karma, which may be summarized as "for every action there is an equal and opposite reaction", is inexorable, unrelenting and immutable. The pain that you inflict upon others will rebound upon you, and the happiness you radiate to another will come back to you, adding to your own happiness.

"By the purity of food, follows the purification of the inner nature."

Swami Sivananda

"Shortly after I began taking classes at the Sivananda Yoga Vedanta Center in America, I read *The Complete Illustrated Book of Yoga* by Swami Vishnu-devananda. Much of it was eye-opening to me, especially the chapter on the 'Natural Diet of Man' (which I assumed included women). I was astonished that the concept of not eating meat had never crossed my mind before. I had never met a vegetarian nor heard of vegetarianism – this was 1962 America.

"One day my mother decided to cook a special treat. She bought some lobsters, filled the bath tub with water so they could await their fate in comfort, and put a big pot of water on to boil. As the live lobsters were dropped into the boiling

water, I heard their screams. The thought crossed my mind, 'How could I cause such unspeakable suffering to my fellow beings, just because I liked the taste of their flesh?' I understood firsthand the yogic principle of ahimsa (non-violence) and never ate meat nor fish again."

Swami Saradananda

The recipes in this book are in accord with the ancient philosophy of Yoga and Vedanta – the non-dualistic philosophy that forms the metaphysical basis of yoga. Yoga prescribes a lacto-vegetarian diet for health and moral and spiritual reasons. This diet is an essential part of yoga, as it promotes a wellness that allows the rest of the discipline to proceed unhampered. A yogic diet is in itself a discipline of both body and mind, and is in accord with the spiritual principle of reverence for life, expressed as ahimsa.

"Purity of food brings purity of mind. Mind is the subtlest essence of food. An aspirant should be careful in the selection of articles of diet in the beginning of his spiritual life."

Swami Sivananda

Annamaya kosha (the physical body) is made of food. Our whole life can be seen as the effect of the interaction of food and life, or matter and energy, which are respectively food and the eater of food. Food is converted into energy, and energy uses food. Food is the door to a healthier life. It helps keep one free of bodily problems so that the mind can concentrate and the spirit can grow. The process of cooking is a good discipline. It involves giving to others, organization, and frequently learning to work under pressure while staying calm. It also encourages cleanliness, imagination and responsibility. The yogic diet consists of pure vegetarian food that is freshly prepared with love. Perhaps as you achieve a proper, healthy diet you will be encouraged to tackle the other four principles of yoga – exercise; breathing; relaxation; and positive thinking and meditation. Even if you are interested only in the physical yoga exercises, you will be surprised by the enhancement of your practice as you modifiy your diet.

The Three Gunas

"Verily, this person consists of the essence of food."

Taittiriya Upanishad, II. 1

In yogic philosophy, the mind is formed from the subtlest portion or essence of food. If the food taken in is pure, the mind has the proper building materials for the development of a strong and subtle intellect and a good memory. A yogic diet is one that brings inner peace to the body and mind and encourages spiritual progress.

All of Nature, including our diet, is catagorized into three qualities, or Gunas: sattvic (pure), rajasic (overstimulating) and tamasic (putrified). A person's mental make-up may be judged from the type of food he/she prefers to eat. Yogis believe not only that 'you are what you eat' but also you eat those foods that reflect your own level of mental and spiritual purity. As your life changes in a positive way, you will also see your food preferences improving. The yogic diet is based on sattvic foods.

Sattvic Foods

"The foods which increase life, purity, strength, health, joy and cheerfulness, which are savoury and oleaginous, substantial and agreeable, are dear to the sattvic people."

Bhagavad Gita, XVII. 8

Pure foods that increase vitality, energy, vigour, health and joy, that are delicious, wholesome, substantial and agreeable are sattvic. These foods render the mind pure and calm and generate equanimity, poise and peaceful tendencies. Sattvic foods supply maximum energy, increase strength and endurance, and help to eliminate fatigue even for those who do strenuous work. They promote a peaceful attitude and are conducive to the practice of meditation.

"Food makes thinking possible. Therefore the right food is of paramount importance. You must eat when you are in a cheerful mood. Do not overload the stomach."

Swami Sivananda

Foods should be as fresh and natural as possible, preferably organically grown, not genetically modified, and kept without preservatives or artificial flavourings. They should also be eaten in as natural a state as possible – either raw, steamed or cooked lightly.

Sattvic foods include:
Grains such as corn, barley, wheat, unpolished rice, oats, millet and quinoa. Make sure you include in your diet coarse foods such as porridge and wholegrain breads. These are good for the teeth and jaws, and they stimulate the processes of digestion and elimination. Grains supply necessary carbohydrates, the main source of energy for the body, and they also contain about half the amino acids (page 68) that are needed to form protein.

Protein foods such as pulses, nuts and seeds. Proteins are the 'building blocks' of the body. The key to a healthy vegetarian diet is to eat a good mixture of foods to ensure that it includes all the amino acids essential for making proteins.

Fruits, both fresh and dried, as well as pure fruit juices, provided the ancient diet of the rishis and raja yogis. Among the many different foods, fruits stand foremost in importance in the yogis' menu or regime. The curative effects of fresh juicy fruits are astonishing. They fill the body with vitalizing, or life-giving, minerals, vitamins and roughage (fibre). They contain alkaline matter that helps to keep the blood pure.

Vegetables are important in the diet because they contain lots of minerals, vitamins and fibre. The diet should include seeded vegetables (such as cucumbers and squashes), all leafy vegetables, and roots or tubers. These are best eaten raw or cooked as lightly as possible.

Herbs for seasoning and herbal teas.

Natural sweeteners, such as honey, molasses, maple syrup and apple juice concentrate, are much better for you than processed sugar. Raw sugar is a traditional part of yogic diets in India, where, known as jaggery, it comes directly from the cane and is not processed. White sugar is best avoided in a healthy diet.

Dairy products, such as milk, butter, cheese and yoghurt, are traditionally an essential part of the yogic diet. However, modern dairy practices abuse the animals, filling their milk with hormones and antibiotics. We have therefore also suggested a vegan alternative for recipes, whenever possible. Even if you choose to use dairy products, we recommend that you do so in moderation. They tend to intensify the production of mucus, which interferes with the natural flow of breath.

Rajasic Foods

"Foods that are bitter, sour, saline, excessively hot, pungent, dry and burning, are liked by the Rajasic and are productive of pain, grief and disease."

Bhagavad Gita, XVII. 9

The yogic diet avoids rajasic foods because they overstimulate the body and mind. They excite passions and boisterous tendencies, cause physical and mental stress, bring a restless state of mind and destroy the mind-body balance that is essential for happiness. However, remember that this division of foods into sattvic-rajasic-tamasic is a comparative one, not an absolute. It is meant to help you gain the insight to change your diet in a positive direction. Hence, spices are used in recipes, but they are used subtly and may be phased out as your tastes become 'sattvic'.

"The modern diet of fast food filled with chemicals and sugar has destroyed the body's natural balance. But yoga can help us to tune back into the body's true needs."

Swami Vishnu-devananda

Onions, garlic, radishes, coffee, tea, tobacco and stimulants of all kind fall into this category – also, heavily spiced and salted, chemical-riddled convenience foods and snacks. Sattvic food taken in the wrong place, i.e. 'on the run', becomes rajasic. Refined (white) sugar, soft drinks, prepared mustards, pungent spices, highly seasoned foods and anything that is excessively hot, bitter, sour or saline are all rajasic and are best avoided.

Strong spices and condiments over-stimulate the mind as well as irritate the mucous membrane of the intestines. Rajasic foods accentuate lust, anger, greed, selfishness, violence and egoism, which are the barriers that separate people from each other and from their realization of the Divine. Rajas is the energy that creates dissension in life and wars in the world.

Tamasic Foods

"That food which is stale, tasteless, putrid, rotten and impure refuse, is the food liked by the Tamasic."

Bhagavad Gita, XVII. 10

Tamasic food makes a person dull, inert and lazy; it robs individuals of high ideals, purpose and motivation. In addition, it accentuates the tendency to suffer from chronic ailments and depression, and fills the minds with darkness, anger and impure thoughts. Abandoning tamasic foods needs to be among the first positive lifestyle changes you make.

Meat, fish, eggs, all intoxicants, alcoholic beverages, marijuana and opium are tamasic in nature. Meat-eating and alcoholism are closely allied. The craving for alcohol dies a natural death when meat is withdrawn from the diet.

Tamasic foods include all foods that are stale, rotten, decomposed, unclean, as well as over-ripe and unripe fruits. Also included are foods that have been fermented, burned, fried, barbecued or reheated many times: half-cooked, over-cooked and twice cooked items, as well as stale products and those containing preservatives, for example canned, processed and many pre-prepared foods.

Mushrooms are included in this category, as they grow in the darkness. Also vinegar, as it is a product of fermentation and retards digestion.

Deep-fried foods are indigestible. The fat penetrates into them and the digestive juice of the stomach cannot act on them. The fine nutritive essence which is beneficial to health is destroyed by frying and the food takes on the quality of tamas.

Sattvic food taken in excessive quantity (overeating) becomes tamasic.

Guidelines for Healthy Eating

"From food all beings are born. Having been born, they grow by food. Food is eaten by all beings and it also eats them."

Taittiriya Upanishad, II. 2. 1

We go on in the circle of birth and death constantly. The body is born, grows, changes, decays, dies ... and is born again. Death means we now have to leave this physical body because of some karma (past action). This body came from food and goes back to the food chain.

Swami Vishnu-devananda illustrates this: "For example, I eat a nice red juicy tomato and my body grows. What happens to the tomato? It changes into my body. And my body itself is also constantly changing. One day it will die. Perhaps when you bury me you will put a tomato plant over the body. The tomato plant will say 'You ate my cousin once upon a time. Now I'm going to eat you.' Then beautiful tomatoes will grow. In this case, destruction of my body is construction of the tomato – and you all enjoy a nice tomato sauce!"

A diet which is not in agreement with the principles of satisfactory nutrition leads to impaired physical development, ill-health and untimely death. A high standard of health, vigour and vitality can be achieved through a well-balanced diet. Such a diet will enable you to develop your inherited capacities to the full extent.

A well-balanced and adequate diet must yield enough calories, as well as supply the various food constituents in sufficient quantities. We need both an energy source for our day-to-day functioning, and vitamins and minerals to stimulate the production of particular hormones and to prevent debilitative diseases.

Simple and natural, non-stimulating tissue-building, energy-producing, non-alcoholic foods and drinks keep the mind calm and pure and help the yogic practitioner to attain the goal of life.

Water is also a necessary part of the diet. About 70 per cent of the body weight is water. There is a daily loss of about 2.5 litres (4½ pints) of water through the skin, lungs, kidneys and the alimentary canal. Water has a greater cleansing action on the tissues than other beverages. It dissolves and distributes food. It is necessary for digestion, and removes impurities from the body. It keeps the body temperature equable through evaporation from the skin in the form of sweat.

Make all changes in your diet gradually. If something disagrees with you, reduce the quantity or eliminate it completely. With practice, you will develop an inner voice to guide you in the selection of a diet suited to your temperament and constitution; one that will maintain your physical efficiency, good health and mental vigour.

Life may be a continual battle, but it is also a never-ending adventure. There are many dragons to be destroyed. You will have to wage war with the enemies of health – impure water, bad ventilation, overwork, unwholesome food, disease-germs, domestic pests such as mosquitoes and flies. We are surrounded on all sides by invisible foes, the pathogenic or disease-causing microbes or bacteria. You should learn all you can about your enemies – their ways, habits and strengths. However, you can also fortify yourself by developing your inner strengths, following these healthy eating guidelines:

- Always respect your food. Begin each meal by giving thanks for it.

- Maintain a peaceful attitude during meals; observe silence if you are alone. When eating with family and friends, try not to argue or discuss unpleasant experiences. Genial conversation can create the balanced, loving environment that enhances digestion and amplifies the body's ability to assimilate the food's nourishment.

- Do not eat when you are angry. Rest for a while until the mind becomes calm and then take some food. Poisons are secreted by the glands and thrown into the bloodstream when you are angry and upset.

- Do not eat food that is too hot, nor too cold, because this will upset the stomach and produce indigestion.

- Do not force yourself to eat anything which you do not like, but also do not eat only those things that you like the most.

- Abandon too many mixtures or combinations of foods. They are difficult for the system to digest. Eat moderately what you find agreeable. Simple diet is best.

- Eat at least one raw dish in each meal to keep your blood alkaline.

- Try to refrain from drinking during a meal as this will dilute the gastric juice, causing indigestion and other stomach complaints.

- Keep the mouth sweet and clean – it is the gate-keeper of the digestive system.

- Eat slowly and savour your food. Chew it thoroughly, remembering that digestion of food begins in the mouth. Appetizing food and thorough chewing stimulate the flow of saliva and other digestive juices.

- Eat moderately. The secret of being healthy and happy is always to be a little hungry. Don't overload the stomach. Overeating hinders elimination, assimilation and growth, making the organs overworked, stressed and vulnerable to disease.

- Gluttons and epicureans cannot even dream of succeeding in yoga. Whoever regulates their diet can become a yogi. Take half a stomachful of food, a quarter stomachful of water and allow the remaining quarter free for the expansion of gas.

Simple, wholesome, pure foods help to neutralize waste material and poisons, and cleanse the system thoroughly.

● Eat at fixed times; try to refrain from eating between meals. If you do not feel hungry at meal time, fast until the next meal. Eat only when you are really hungry. Beware of false hunger. The gastric fire is God. Wait for the appearance of this God within and only then offer some food.

● Try to eat as little processed food as possible.

● Foods are best when cooked lightly. Over-cooking robs them of their nutritional value and flavour.

● Try not to eat large meals late at night. Do not eat rice or beans at this time, as they are heavy to digest and you will find it difficult to get up for meditation in the morning. If you are very hungry, eat something light – perhaps some fruit.

● Eat to live, don't live to eat. You need food to maintain body heat, produce new cells and repair wear and tear. Be simple in your eating habits. The person who practises regular meditation wants very little food.

● Take some lemon and honey in the morning for health and energy, and to purify the blood.

"Moderate diet is defined to mean taking pleasant and sweet food, leaving one-fourth of the stomach free, and offering the act up to the Lord."

Hatha Yoga Pradipika, I. 58

● Do not practise asanas immediately after eating, nor when you are hungry. Also, it is not advisable to do any strenuous physical or mental work immediately after eating. In the morning, when physical and nervous forces are at their most vigorous, the stomach can proceed with its functions if the breakfast is followed by moderate exercise, such as a leisurely walk to the bus. After supper there should be no work, but recreation. Bodily vigour is at its lowest and should not be taxed further.

● Try sitting in Vajra Asana (sitting on the heels with knees and feet together) for 10 minutes after a meal; this will assist digestion.

● Do not become a slave to food and drink. Do not make much fuss about diet. Take simple and natural foods. If you think too much about food this will create more body-consciousness.

● Try fasting one day per week. Fasting eliminates poisons, overhauls the internal mechanism and gives rest to the organs.

● Remember God, the indweller of all foods, the bestower of all bounties. Remember God during meals and give thanks to God just before and after eating.

"We are constantly bombarded with stimuli, and these make up the diet of our lifestyle. From the food we eat, the air we breath, the things we see, feel, hear and touch our environment is formed and this in turn profoundly influences and shapes our internal environment. We are what we eat – literally, for the mind is constructed out of the sublest parts of our diet and the body from the rest. To achieve the goal of life, to find contentment and perfection requires a peaceful and focused mind. To control the mind is difficult since it is in reality very much under the control of our physical body. It is therefore suggested that we first discipline and control the physical body and then the mind may be easily controlled. Diet plays an important part in this process."

Swami Vishnu-devananda

Replacement Foods

The following are substitutions that you can use in standard recipes to help you to make a gradual change to a yogic diet.

Food	Yogic replacement
Cheese, grated	*Yeast flakes*
Cottage cheese	*Tofu, crumbled*
Eggs – as binder	*1 tablespoon peanut butter, tahini or blended tofu per egg or 1 teaspoon soya flour*
Eggs – as leavening agent	*Baking powder or yoghurt plus sparkling mineral water*
Eggs – as protein source	*Tofu (plus a pinch of turmeric, if desired)*
Flesh foods	*Tofu, tempeh, pulses (beans)*
Golden syrup	*Barley malt syrup*
Milk	*Soya milk, nut and seed milks, oat milk, rice milk*
Onions	*Cabbage, celery or turnips*
Vinegar	*Lemon juice*

Making Positive Changes in Your Life

Eating a wholesome diet is a very good start to making positive changes; it is the opening of a door to a healthier and happier way of life. Some changes may seem easy, but others take a bit longer. The following suggestions, combined with yoga exercises, will help you make the positive changes permanent. Yoga sessions begin with a few minutes relaxation in the Corpse pose. The asanas begin with the Sun Salutation, a warming-up exercise. OM is the original mantra, the root of all sounds and letters (see Glossary, page 156).

	1-7 weeks	2-6 months	6 months-1 year	2-3 years	Continuing on
Proper exercise	12 Basic asanas + Sun Salutation.	Add simple variations.	Add Intermediate variations.	Intermediate/ Advanced asanas.	Advanced asanas.
Proper breathing	Practise deep abdominal breathing.	Learn basic pranayama.	Practise 15-30min. pranayama daily.	Practise 30min. pranayama daily.	Practise 30-45min. pranayama daily.
Proper relaxation	Learn Corpse pose.	Relax in Corpse pose 15min. daily.	Relax in Corpse pose 15min. daily.	Relax in Corpse pose 15min. daily.	Relax in Corpse pose 15min. daily.
Reduce negative dietary habits	Eliminate meat and fish from your diet. Cut down on fried foods.	Eliminate eggs from your diet. Cut down on soft drinks and sweets.	Cut down on heavily salted and convenience foods.	Eliminate stale, burned and tamasic foods.	Eliminate onions, garlic and other rajasic foods from your diet.
Re-inforcing positive dietary habits	Drink 4-5 glasses of water daily and eat one raw salad daily.	Increase intake of pulses and tofu.	Eat food that is as freshly prepared as possible.	Eat at least one meal per week in silence.	Practise thankfulness at each meal.
Fasting	Replace one meal each week with a glass of freshly made juice.	Fast on water or fresh juices for one day each week.	Once a year, do a 3-day fast on water or fresh juices. Practise kriyas.	Once or twice a year do a 3-day fast on water or fresh juices.	Fast twice a year: once, for a week, on vegetable juices; for the other, do 3 days on water.
Eradicating negative habits	If you use marijuana or any other drugs, replace them with abdominal breathing.	Stop smoking. Whenever you want a cigarette, do yogic breathing.	Cut down and eventually eliminate the intake of alcohol.	Begin to cut down on consumption of of coffee, tea and other stimulants.	Evaluate your bad habits and try to eliminate them, one by one.
Concentration exercises	Let go of the past and future, focusing only in the present.	Practise listening and hearing what others are saying.	Practise tratak (candle gazing exercise) daily.	Mentally repeat 'OM' or other mantra 10min. daily.	Practise focusing on one thing at a time.
Positive thinking	Refrain from using abusive language.	Try to spend time with people who have a positive outlook on life.	Stop procrastinating. Put positive ideas into practice as soon as possible.	Remove words like 'can't' from your vocabulary (including your mental vocabulary).	Begin to see your failures as stepping stones to success; view as learning experiences.
Meditation	Sit silently for at least 20 min. daily with the mind focused on breath.	Mentally repeat a mantra, such as 'OM', tuning it to the breath.	Increase your time of sitting to 30min. daily.	With regular practice, the mind becomes less jumpy.	Continue the regular practice and you will experience peace.
Study	Read something of inspiration daily.	Study some verses of scripture or poetry that are uplifting by nature.	Develop a contemplative attitude by seeing how these verses apply to your life.	Attend discourses or workshops that discuss inspirational readings.	Continue to study daily, trying to put it into practice in your daily life.

A Prayer Before Meals

ब्रह्मार्पणं ब्रह्महविर्ब्रह्माग्नौ ब्रह्मणा हुतम् ।
ब्रह्मैव तेन गन्तव्यं ब्रह्मकर्मसमाधिना ॥ २४ ॥

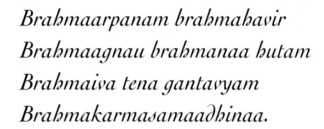

Brahmaarpanam brahmahavir
Brahmaagnau brahmanaa hutam
Brahmaiva tena gantavyam
Brahmakarmasamaadhinaa.

Brahman is the oblation
Brahman is the offering
By Brahman is the oblation poured into the fire of Brahman
Brahman verily shall be reached
By the person who sees Brahman in all and sees Brahman in all action.
Bhagavad Gita, IV. 24

The process of eating is Brahman
The offering (the food itself) is Brahman
The person (the eater) who is doing the offering (the eating) is Brahman,
and the (gastric) fire by which the food is consumed is also Brahman
Thus by seeing Brahman everywhere in action, one reaches that Divine State
(Brahman).

YOGIC START
TO THE DAY

"Be sober and temperate; you will be healthy. Bask in the sun; spend time in the open air. The sun and the open air are your good doctor. Let your food be simple. Never eat too much, but don't eat too little. Take sufficient exercise. Become your own physician."

Swami Sivananda

A much neglected meal, breakfast all too often consists of a quick bowl of boxed cereal and hasty cup(s) of coffee. As most nutritionists emphasize that this is the most important meal of the day, we include a range of healthy recipes that can be prepared with a minimum of fuss, to set you up for the day.

Breakfast can be a light or more substantial meal depending on your eating patterns, but it is best not to miss it. Eating a healthy breakfast makes it less likely that you will capitulate to unhealthy mid-morning snacks or be so ravenous by lunch time that you overeat. Children, in particular, need a proper breakfast otherwise they tend to become listless and have difficulty concentrating.

In Sivananda ashrams (monasteries or quiet places where one practises yoga) around the world the daily routine includes two substantial meals, to fit in with the programme of asanas and meditation. Breakfast is taken at 10 am after morning meditation and asanas. Usually everyone is ready for a substantial meal by this time, especially as the next meal is served at 6 pm.

The morning meal, more than any other, reminds us of the essential function of food – to fuel our bodies. When most of us think of breakfast, only a few foods and beverages come to mind. But here we offer an interesting and health-filled variety to choose from. As with all meals, the good breakfast should strike a balance between the different categories of food. Whole grains, in the form of cereals, breads or pancakes, provide a rich source of complex carbohydrates. The inclusion of fruits satisfies the longing for sweetness. Protein in the form of tofu or pulses helps to raise the basal metabolic rate, giving a feeling of energy and well-being.

Ginger Carrot Juice

Starting with natural raw foods gives you stamina and energy to cope with the stress and strains of the day. Carrots are a good tonic for the brain, rich in vitamin A and minerals such as calcium. As well as nourishing the body in general, this juice will clear the lungs. The warming properties of ginger improve circulation and help the prana to flow freely. This is wonderful when you are on a juice fast. The apples or celery can be omitted, if preferred, and you can vary the amount of ginger according to personal taste. About 200g (7oz) of roughly chopped cabbage may be substituted for the apples. Use organic carrots and apples, if possible; if they are not organic, peel them. Serves 4

2 crisp, juicy eating apples, quartered
3 carrots, scrubbed
1 stick of celery

1-2.5cm (½-1in) piece of fresh root ginger, peeled, or a pinch of ground ginger
200ml (7fl oz) water
juice of ½ a lemon or 1 whole lime

1 If you have a juicer, use it to juice the apples, carrots, celery and piece of root ginger. Alternatively, chop the carrots and celery, place in a food processor with the apples and ginger and process to a pulp, then press out the juice through a fine sieve.

2 Dilute the juice with the water. Stir in the lemon or lime juice and the ground ginger, if using. Serve at once.

Minty Tomato Juice

A refreshing and cleansing early morning drink. However, tomatoes are too acidic to use while fasting. The combined warming effect of the tomato, lime and cayenne pepper makes a wonderful tonic for winter. Fresh juices are the most vital and regenerating of foods, containing readily available energy to nourish the cells of the body. Serves 4-6

1 litre (1¾ pints) tomato juice
3 tablespoons fresh lime juice
2 tablespoons finely chopped fresh mint

pinch of cayenne pepper (optional)
lime slices, to garnish

Combine the tomato juice, lime juice, mint and cayenne pepper, if using. Pour into individual glasses and serve as soon as possible, garnished with lime slices.

Almond Milk
This sustaining and soothing drink was developed by Swami Vishnu-devananda during the time that he was doing intensive sadhana (yogic practice) in the Himalayas. It is served daily during the Sivananda Sadhana intensive courses which are run for yoga teachers, as it is a rich source of easily digestible food for the rapid replenishment of energy. Almonds are a concentrated source of protein, as well as being high in vitamins and minerals such as iron, magnesium, potassium and zinc. The fat content makes them excellent for skin and muscle repair. Highly valued in Ayurveda (the traditional Indian medical system), almonds strengthen the respiratory system and lubricate the intestines. The ingredients below are per person, simply multiply them by the number of people you want to serve. Recipe per person

10 almonds, soaked overnight in enough
   water to cover
pinch of ground cardamom

pinch of pepper
250ml (8fl oz) warm milk, water or soya milk
1 teaspoon honey

1 Drain the almonds, reserving the soaking water, and remove the skins. Place the nuts in a food processor or blender with the soaking water and the cardamom and pepper. Blend at high speed for 5 minutes.

2 Combine the almond mixture with the warm milk, water or soya milk. Stir in the honey. Drink at once.

Citrus Slices with Pomegranate Seeds
An attractive fruit salad such as this one is the perfect way to brighten a grey morning! The pomegranate seeds invigorate the system while cooling and strengthening it, and they are an excellent blood purifier. The ginger gives the salad some bite, as well as stimulating the digestion. Serves 4-6

1 orange
1 pink grapefruit
1-2 kiwi fruit (optional)

½ a pomegranate
1 tablespoon finely chopped crystallized
   ginger (optional)

1 Peel the citrus fruit and slice into 6mm (¼in) thick rounds or divide into segments, removing as much pith as possible. Slice or quarter the kiwi fruit, if using.

2 Arrange the fruit on a serving platter. Scoop out the pomegranate seeds with a spoon, omitting the pulp around them. Sprinkle the pomegranate seeds and chopped crystallized ginger, if using, over the top of the fruit. Serve at once.

• If pomegranate seeds are not available, use black grapes to add colour to this dish.
• Substitute chopped fresh mint leaves for the crystallized ginger.
• Fresh sliced pineapple is also a welcome ingredient.

Apple Fig Salad Serves 6

6 dried or fresh figs
2 eating apples and 2 bananas, sliced
200g (7oz) chopped walnuts
2 tablespoons grated unsweetened coconut

1 tablespoon lemon juice
4 tablespoons clear honey
125ml (4fl oz) yoghurt, crème fraîche or Toasted
  Nut Dream (page 115) (optional)

If using dried figs, soak them in cold water for 1-2 hours, then drain. Cut the fresh or dried figs into quarters. Mix the fruit, chopped nuts, grated coconut, lemon juice and honey together. Serve at once, topped with yoghurt, crème fraîche or toasted nut dream, if desired.

Baked Bananas *There is an old Indian folk saying: "Bananas are gold in the morning, silver at noon and lead at night." Their high carbohydrate content makes them the perfect breakfast food for an active lifestyle and their potassium content encourages muscle pliancy – if you suffer from muscle cramps, bananas will help to alleviate them. The students at our yoga centres and ashrams consume vast amounts of the fruit for this reason.* Serves 4-8

4 bananas
125ml (4fl oz) maple syrup
125ml (4fl oz) orange juice
50g (2oz) chopped or flaked almonds

¼ teaspoon ground cardamom
50g (2oz) butter or margarine, melted
a little grated fresh coconut or toasted
  desiccated coconut for sprinkling (optional)

1 Preheat the oven to 200°C/400°F/Gas mark 6. Peel the bananas and halve them lengthwise. Lay them in a baking dish.

2 Combine the maple syrup, orange juice, almonds, cardamom and melted butter or margarine. Pour the mixture over the bananas and bake in the oven for 30 minutes. Serve at once, topped with grated or toasted coconut, if desired.

Winter Compote Serves 4-6

200g (7oz) dried apricots
100g (4oz) prunes
100g (4oz) dried pears
100g (4oz) dried apples

6 cloves
1 cinnamon stick
1 tablespoon apple juice concentrate
600ml (1 pint) water

1 Place the dried fruit in a bowl with the spices, apple juice concentrate and water and leave to soak overnight.

2 The next morning, transfer the mixture to a pan and bring to the boil. Reduce the heat, half cover the pan and simmer for 25 minutes. Remove the spices and serve.

• **Winter Fruit Shake:** If you don't have time to prepare the compote, you can make it into this quick shake, which combines the nourishment of dried fruits with protein-rich soya milk for a wonderful morning energy booster. Omit the cloves, cinnamon stick, apple juice concentrate and water. Place the dried fruits (it doesn't matter whether they are soaked or not) in a food processor or blender with 250-500ml (8-18fl oz) soya milk (or milk, if preferred). Add ½ teaspoon ground cinnamon, if desired. Blend until smooth and serve.

Granola

There are many recipes for granola. This one contains no added oil, but includes a wonderful array of grains, nuts and seeds – a veritable treasure house of natural oils, minerals and vitamins! At our Yoga Retreat on Paradise Island, Bahamas, we pick fresh coconuts off the trees. When opened, the coconut pulp is shredded and 50g (2oz) is toasted along with the grain mixture. Dried coconut may be used as a variation. If adding coconut, the liquid sweetener may be reduced. You can simplify the recipe by increasing the quantities of some ingredients if you do not have others. Granola can be made in advance and then stored in an airtight container in a cool place (not the refrigerator) for several weeks. To serve, simply add some milk, yoghurt or soya milk. Makes about 12-16 servings

175ml (6fl oz) maple syrup
125ml (4fl oz) hot water
½ teaspoon vanilla essence
300g (10oz) rolled oats
150g (5oz) rye, millet or wheat flakes
50g (2oz) wheatgerm or bran

100g (4oz) hazelnuts, almonds or any other nuts
75g (3oz) sunflower seeds
50g (2oz) sesame seeds
75g (3oz) sultanas or raisins
50g (2oz) chopped dates or other dried fruits (optional)

1 Preheat the oven to 120°C/250°F/Gas mark ½. Combine the maple syrup, hot water and vanilla essence.

2 Mix the grains, nuts and seeds in a large mixing bowl. Stir in the maple syrup and vanilla solution and mix thoroughly. Spread out the mixture on a lightly oiled baking sheet and bake in the oven for about 1 hour, stirring three or four times to prevent it from burning. The granola is ready when it is lightly browned.

3 Mix the granola with the dried fruit while still warm, breaking up the larger chunks as you do so. Leave to cool and then store in airtight containers.

Oatmeal Yoghurt Cream

The Sivananda Yoga International Headquarters is in maple syrup-producing Quebec, Canada, so we always have supplies on hand. However, if you don't have ready access, you can use barley malt syrup, rice syrup, date syrup or honey. Serves 3-4 people

50g (2oz) almonds, finely chopped
50g (2oz) medium oatmeal (not flakes)
grated rind and juice of ½ a lemon or orange

2 tablespoons maple syrup or sweetener of choice
300ml (10fl oz) creamy natural yoghurt
1 tablespoon chopped almonds, toasted

1 Preheat the grill. Mix together the chopped almonds and oatmeal. Spread out on a baking sheet and place under the hot grill for about 2 minutes, stirring frequently to brown evenly. Leave to cool.

2 Mix the lemon or orange rind and juice with the sweetener and stir into the yoghurt. Fold in the almond mixture. Spoon into individual glass dishes and chill until required.

3 Top with toasted chopped almonds and serve at once.

Apple Muesli

A quick and easy recipe for when time is short. Oats are renowned for their energy-giving properties as well as the warmth they give to the body. Because they are very alkaline, they relieve tension and help you to practise 'proper relaxation'. Serves 4-6

50g (2oz) raisins
150ml (5fl oz) unsweetened apple juice
2 eating apples, cored and coarsely chopped
250g (9oz) rolled oats

1 tablespoon honey
25g (1oz) flaked almonds
milk, yoghurt or soya milk, to serve

1 Soak the raisins in the apple juice for 20 minutes. Put the chopped apples into a bowl, add the raisins and apple juice and toss to combine them.

2 Stir in the oats and honey. Add the almonds and stir well to mix everything together. Serve at once with milk, yoghurt or soya milk.

• Double the amount of the apple juice; soak the raisins and oats overnight. Add the other ingredients in the morning.

Orange Couscous

For a refreshingly different start to the day, try this dish instead of porridge. In summer, fresh apricots or peaches can be used. The toasted coconut provides a rich texture to the dish, which can be served plain or with yoghurt, milk or soya milk. Serves 4-6

12 dried apricots, thinly sliced
500ml (18fl oz) orange juice
¼ teaspoon salt
175g (6oz) couscous

3 tablespoons grated fresh or desiccated
coconut, toasted
1 orange, peeled and divided into
segments, to serve (optional)

1 Place the apricots, orange juice and salt in a saucepan and bring to the boil. Stir in the couscous and remove from the heat. Cover the pan and let it stand for 5 minutes, until the liquid has been absorbed by the couscous. The couscous should be light and fluffy, and slightly grainy to the bite.

2 Place in individual serving bowls. Top each portion with a little toasted coconut and orange segments, if desired. Serve warm.

• **Apple Cinnamon Bulgar:** Put 2 roughly chopped crisp eating apples, 500ml (18fl oz) unsweetened apple juice, 50g (2oz) raisins or sultanas, ¼ teaspoon ground cinnamon and ¼ teaspoon salt into a saucepan and bring to the boil. Stir in 200g (7oz) bulgar wheat. Cover and simmer over a low heat for about 15 minutes, until all the liquid has been absorbed. Serve warm, sprinkled with chopped nuts or sunflower seeds.

Uppama with Mixed Vegetables *A South Indian*

breakfast or supper dish. Serve with Coconut Chutney (page 125) or yoghurt. Serves 6

450g (1lb) coarse semolina
300g (10oz) potatoes, diced
3/4 teaspoon paprika and 3/4 teaspoon turmeric
salt
125ml (4fl oz) oil
1½ teaspoons black mustard seeds
1½ teaspoons cumin seeds
3 tomatoes, chopped

4cm (1½in) piece fresh root ginger, peeled
and finely chopped
3 fresh green chillies, seeded and
finely chopped (optional)
300g (10oz) mixed vegetables (carrots, cabbage,
green pepper), very finely chopped or grated
750ml (1¼ pints) boiling water
a few sprigs of fresh coriander leaves, chopped

1 Heat a large frying pan or wok, add the semolina, and cook over a low heat for 10-12 minutes, until it is a few shades darker, stirring constantly. Remove from the pan and set aside.

2 Sprinkle the potatoes with paprika, turmeric and a little salt. Heat the oil in the frying pan, add the potatoes and sauté over a medium heat until brown. Remove with a slotted spoon; set aside.

3 Add the mustard and cumin seeds to the frying pan and heat them over a high heat until they begin to 'pop'. Add the tomatoes, ginger and chillies, if using, and stir well over a low heat. Add the mixed vegetables and cook for 5 minutes.

4 Add the boiling water and 1 teaspoon salt. Gradually add the roasted semolina, stirring all the time. The mixture should be light and crumbly with no lumps. Add a little more water if the mixture is too dry. Gently mix in the fried potatoes, and garnish with coriander leaves. Serve at once.

Dosas *These light crêpes are a typical breakfast in South India. The rice and urid dal (a type of white lentil available from Indian food stores) combine to make perfectly balanced protein. Serve with Coconut Chutney (page 125) and Sambar (page 140). Or stuff with Curried Potato (page 88) to make Masala Dosa.* Serves 4-6

150g (5oz) urid dal, washed
300g (10oz) basmati rice
800ml (28fl oz) water

1 teaspoon crushed fenugreek (optional)
1 teaspoon salt
ghee or oil for cooking

1 Place the urid dal and rice in separate bowls. Add 300ml (10fl oz) of the water to the urid dal and stir in the fenugreek, if using. Add the rest of the water to the rice. Leave to soak for at least 12 hours, then grind them separately in a food processor or blender with the water they have been soaked in, grinding until smooth, adding a little more water if necessary. Combine the urid dal and rice to make a runny batter. Leave to stand in a warm place for 8 hours, or overnight – it will get slightly thicker and fizzy overnight.

2 Heat a heavy frying pan or griddle over a medium heat and grease very lightly with oiled paper towel. Stir the salt into the batter, which should be a thick, pouring consistency. Drop a ladleful of batter (about 3 tablespoons) into the pan. Using the back of the ladle, very gently swirl the batter from the centre outwards to make a thin, crêpe-like dosa.

3 Cook over a medium heat until the edges of the dosa start to lift (1-3 minutes). Brush very lightly with ghee or oil and turn it over – if you try and turn it over too soon before it has started to set, the dosa will break. Cook until golden brown. Serve at once.

Dosas with Curried Potato and Coconut Chutney

Wheat-free Crêpes

For breakfast or a snack, these light, crispy crêpes are so good that they can be served plain or with maple syrup. For a festive breakfast, serve them hot with Baked Bananas (page 24). They can also be filled with either a sweet or savoury filling, folded and topped with syrup or a sauce. Serves 4-6

100g (4oz) soya flour
225g (8oz) rice flour
3 teaspoons baking powder
pinch of salt
350ml (12fl oz) water

1-2 teaspoons honey
4 tablespoons oil
oil for frying
maple syrup or Raisin Sauce (page 114), to serve

1 Combine the soya flour, rice flour, baking powder and salt. Add the water a little at a time, stirring so that the mixture is smooth. Gradually beat in the honey and the oil – the mixture should be quite runny.

2 Heat a heavy frying pan over a high heat, reduce to a medium heat and brush with oil. Add a ladleful of mixture to the pan and flatten out thinly with the back of a spoon. Fry until the centre bubbles, turn it over and cook until golden brown. Repeat with the remaining mixture to make 10-12 crêpes. Serve hot, with maple syrup or raisin sauce.

• Buckwheat Pancakes: This traditional American favourite is frequently served on Sunday morning at our Catskill Mountain Yoga Ranch in New York State. Combine 150g (5oz) wholewheat flour, 75g (3oz) buckwheat flour, 40g (1½oz) powdered milk and 1 teaspoon baking powder in a mixing bowl. Gradually add enough water to give a runny consistency, then beat in 4 tablespoons molasses, 2 tablespoons natural yoghurt and 2 tablespoons oil. Cook spoonfuls of the mixture to make chunkier pancakes 10-12.5cm (4-5in) in diameter. Cook three or four at a time. As each pancake is removed from the pan, top with a pat of butter and place the next pancake on top, repeating the layers to make a stack of four to six pancakes per person. Pour on maple syrup or Raisin Sauce (page 114) made with a little extra water. Each person gets a stack. To eat, the stacks are sliced like a cake and eaten slice by slice, rather than pancake by pancake.

Fruit Toast

An interesting departure from the more traditional cinnamon toast. This recipe needs a little preparation but is a wonderfully satisfying weekend breakfast. Any seasonal fruit may be used. Recipe per person

1 teaspoon butter or margarine
1 peach, nectarine or apple, or 2 apricots, sliced
2 teaspoons sugar-free whole fruit apricot or peach jam

1 teaspoon lemon juice (optional)
1 slice light rye or sunflower seed bread, lightly toasted

1 Preheat the oven to 200°C/400°F/Gas mark 6. Melt the butter or margarine in a large, heavy-based saucepan or frying pan and sauté the fruit for 2-3 minutes, until it begins to soften. Turn off the heat and stir in the fruit jam and lemon juice, if using.

2 Place the toast on a baking sheet and spoon the fruit mixture on top of it. Bake in the oven for 5-10 minutes and serve immediately.

Carrot and Molasses Muffins
Special thanks go to Martha and to Swami Premananda for these recipes. Muffins should come out of the oven nicely golden with a moist centre. Problems are usually caused by the mixture being too dry or too wet; if necessary, add more water, oil or flour to bring it to a wet and sticky consistency (not runny), but take care not to overmix the ingredients or the muffins will be heavy. The correct consistency is like mud. For richer muffins, replace some of the water with milk or soya milk. Buttermilk is especially good, as it helps the muffins to rise. These muffins are made with finely ground wholewheat flour called wholewheat pastry flour, available from health food stores. Makes 12 large muffins

250g (9oz) finely grated raw carrots or
   450g (1lb) mashed cooked carrots
450g (1lb) wholewheat pastry flour
100g (4oz) soya flour
1 teaspoon ground cinnamon

400g (14oz) chopped dates
200g (7oz) chopped nuts (optional)
125ml (4fl oz) molasses
175m (6fl oz) oil
4 tablespoons water

1 Preheat the oven to 180°C/350°F/Gas mark 4. Combine the raw or cooked carrots, flours, cinnamon, dates, and nuts, if using. Mix the molasses, oil and water in a separate large bowl.

2 Add the molasses and oil mixture to the carrot mixture and fold together quickly until all the dry ingredients are moistened and evenly mixed.

3 Spoon into greased muffin tins and bake in the oven for 20-30 minutes, until a fine skewer or fork inserted into the centre of a muffin comes out clean.

Savoury Cheese Muffins
Makes 12 large muffins

200g (7oz) vegetarian Cheddar cheese, grated
2 teaspoons dried oregano
600g (1¼lb) wholewheat flour
100g (4oz) carrots, grated
100g (4oz) courgette, finely chopped, or green
   pepper, cored, seeded and finely chopped

100g (4oz) canned sweetcorn kernels
1 teaspoon dried basil
3 teaspoons baking powder
1 teaspoon salt and ¼ teaspoon pepper
500ml (18fl oz) soya milk or buttermilk
250ml (8fl oz) oil

1 Preheat the oven to 180°C/350°F/Gas mark 4. Set aside 50g (2oz) of the grated cheese and 1 teaspoon of the oregano. Combine all the rest of the ingredients, except the soya milk or buttermilk and oil, in a bowl. In a separate large bowl, mix the milk and oil together.

2 Add the milk and oil mixture to the dry mixture and fold together quickly until the dry ingredients are moistened and evenly mixed.

3 Spoon into greased muffin tins. Mix the reserved cheese and oregano together and sprinkle it over the top of the muffins. Bake in the oven for 20-30 minutes, until a fine skewer or fork inserted into the centre of a muffin comes out clean.

• For a vegan version, use soya cheese.
• For a wheat-free version, replace the wheat flour with buckwheat or spelt flour.
• Substitute cornmeal for half the wholewheat flour.
• Use other fresh or dried herb combinations of your choice.

SOUP
SAMSKARAS

*"Eat moderately what you know
by experience is agreeable to you
and what is digestible.
Simple diet is best."*

Swami Sivananda

'Samskaras' are the subtle impressions formed in the conscious and subconscious minds by our daily activities and experiences. When the body is properly nourished, samskaras of strength are imprinted and we feel better able to deal with the stresses of life.

At the start of a meal, or as a main meal in itself, soups are nutritious, satisfying and easy to prepare. Nothing is more warming or fulfilling than a hearty bowl of soup on a cold day – it nourishes both body and soul. On a warm summer's day, a refreshing light soup rejuvenates the mind and invigorates the prana. Soups can be an innovative and economical way to feed a family or group of friends using simple ingredients and techniques. Soups can also be an easy yet substantial meal for people with busy lives.

Basic Vegetable Soup

The variations on this basic theme are endless. In winter, root vegetables, such as parsnips, turnips and swedes, make a grounding, warming soup base. In the summer, lighter greens may be substituted, along with fresh herbs. This is an easy soup to make for any number of people. For a stronger flavour, add one bay leaf per four people with the vegetables. The ingredients below are for one person; simply multiply them by the number of people you want to feed. Recipe per person

50g (2oz) mixed vegetables (celery, courgettes, carrots, turnips, swede, potatoes)
½ tablespoon oil or 7g (¼oz) butter (optional)
250ml (8fl oz) water

sea salt or tamari to taste
chopped parsley or coriander, to garnish (optional)

1 Clean the vegetables; dice or slice attractively.

2 If liked, heat the oil or butter in a pan and sauté the mixed vegetables until they are slightly softened.

3 Place the water in a large pan or soup pot and bring to the boil. Add the vegetables. Lower the heat, cover and simmer for 20 minutes.

4 Season with tamari or sea salt, and serve garnished with chopped parsley or coriander.

• **Blended Vegetable Soup:** After cooking, transfer the soup to a food processor or blender and purée it until smooth. Return it to the pan and heat through. Serve garnished with parsley or coriander.

• **Hearty Vegetable Soup:** Pulses may be pre-soaked, added to the water and cooked until almost soft before adding the vegetables.

• **Spring Vegetable Soup:** For each person, add 25g (1oz) seasonal greens, such as sorrel, spinach, dandelion or watercress, or 3 tablespoons chopped fresh herbs, such as basil, fennel, dill or tarragon, to the soup before seasoning it. Cook for a further 5 minutes and then season with sea salt or tamari.

• **Creamy Vegetable Soup:** Replace some of the water with milk or soya milk. Do this towards the end of the cooking as milk/soya milk should not be boiled but only heated. Alternatively, add 1-2 tablespoons cream or yoghurt per person before serving.

• **Creamy Vegan Soup:** For each person, sauté 1 tablespoon rolled oats with the chopped vegetables. This makes a light, creamy, nourishing soup.

Winter Warming Soup
This variation of Basic Vegetable Soup (see left) is transformed into a hearty meal by adding barley, which is a wonderful aid to the digestive system and, when combined with warming spices, makes the perfect soup to counteract the winter cold. Use high-fibre wholegrain pot barley rather than pearl barley. Serves 6-8

3 tablespoons oil
4 sticks of celery, finely chopped
4 carrots, chopped into bite-sized cubes
1 small swede, chopped into bite-sized cubes
2 litres (3½ pints) boiling water
2 bay leaves
100g (4oz) pot barley

1 teaspoon ground cumin
1 teaspoon ground coriander
½ teaspoon pepper
sea salt to taste
1 tablespoon chopped fresh parsley
   or coriander

1 Heat the oil in a large pan, add the celery and sauté for 2 minutes. Add the carrots and swede and continue cooking for another 5 minutes.

2 Add the water, bay leaves, barley and ground cumin and coriander. Simmer for 30 minutes, or until the vegetables and barley are soft.

3 Remove half the soup and purée it in a food processor or blender until smooth. Return it to the pan and season with the pepper and salt. Reheat, then serve at once, garnished with the chopped parsley or coriander.

Carrot Soup
Traditionally, orange or saffron-colour symbolizes the fire of renunciation by which all karma (past action) is burnt. In this vibrant soup, the orange juice and fresh mint lighten the earthy quality of the carrots. Serves 4-6

25g (1oz) butter or margarine
600g (1¼lb) carrots, grated
500ml (18fl oz) water

500ml (18fl oz) orange juice
salt and pepper
2 tablespoons chopped fresh mint

1 Heat the butter or margarine in a large pan and sauté the carrots until they begin to soften. Add the water, half cover and simmer over a low to medium heat for about 20 minutes, until the carrots are soft.

2 Remove from the heat and allow to cool slightly. Place the carrots and cooking water in a food processor or blender, add the orange juice and purée the mixture until smooth. Alternatively, press through a large sieve.

3 Return the soup to the pan, season to taste with salt and pepper and reheat without boiling. Serve garnished with the chopped mint.

• Omit the orange juice and double the quantity of water. Replace the chopped mint with a pinch of freshly grated nutmeg.

Nutty Parsnip Soup

As warm and comforting as it is unusual, this recipe was devised by Stephen Cooke, one of our guest chefs, who has since returned to Australia. The peanut butter adds body to the soothing almost apple-like sweetness of the parsnips. Serves 4-6

2 carrots, chopped
2 sticks of celery, chopped
3 parsnips, chopped
1 tablespoon fresh thyme or coriander leaves

1.5 litres (2¾ pints) water
1-2 tablespoons crunchy peanut butter
salt or tamari
squeeze of lemon juice (optional)

1 Place the vegetables in a large pan with the herbs and water. Bring to the boil, half cover and simmer for 15-20 minutes, until the vegetables are soft.

2 Allow to cool slightly, then transfer to a food processor or blender, add the peanut butter and blend until smooth.

3 Return the purée to the pan. Season to taste with salt or tamari and add a little lemon juice, if desired. Reheat without boiling and serve at once.

Roasted Tomato Soup

Simple wholesome, pure foods like this soup help to maintain physical health and mental equilibrium. Try to use ripe red tomatoes, though the grated carrot ensures that whatever tomatoes you use the soup will not be too tart. Roasting the tomatoes first adds an exotic flavour to the soup.
Serves 4-6

450g (1lb) tomatoes
2 tablespoons oil
1 red pepper, cored, seeded and chopped
1 carrot, grated
2 sticks of celery, sliced
1 tablespoon chopped fresh oregano or
¾ teaspoon dried

1 tablespoon torn fresh basil or 1 teaspoon dried
750ml (1¼ pints) hot water
1 teaspoon salt
¼ teaspoon pepper
basil and oregano leaves, or 2 tablespoons
chopped fresh parsley, to garnish

1 Preheat the oven to 200°C/400°F/Gas mark 6 and roast the whole tomatoes, turning frequently until the skins fall away (about 15 minutes). Cool slightly, then peel and chop them.

2 Heat the oil in a pan and sauté the pepper, carrot and celery over a medium heat for a few minutes. Add the oregano and basil, stir well and cook for a few more minutes.

3 Add the water and tomatoes. Season with salt and pepper. Half cover and simmer for about 20 minutes. Transfer to a food processor or blender and blend for a few seconds. Return the soup to the pan and reheat if necessary, then serve garnished with fresh basil and oregano leaves or chopped parsley.

• For a thicker consistency, add 200g (7oz) chopped cooked potatoes to the vegetables.
• For an even heartier soup, add some cooked grain 10 minutes before the end of the cooking time.
• For a creamier soup, add a little soya milk or cream just before serving.

Borscht
A native dish from Eastern Europe, borscht can be served as either a summer or winter soup. When the temperature drops, serve the soup with a plate of boiled potatoes for a satisfying supper. Beetroot is an excellent blood tonic. Serves 6-8

1 tablespoon oil
1 stick of celery, chopped
1 bay leaf
4 raw beetroot, scrubbed and chopped into bite-sized pieces
1 carrot, grated
1 potato, chopped into bite-sized pieces
2 litres (3½ pints) water
100g (4oz) beet tops, spinach or kale, chopped (optional)

juice of ½ a lemon
1 teaspoon salt
pinch of pepper
pinch of paprika
1 teaspoon fresh dill or ¼ teaspoon dried dill weed
soured cream, soya cream or yoghurt, to serve
finely chopped fresh parsley, to garnish

1 Heat the oil in a large pan and sauté the chopped celery until soft. Add the bay leaf, beetroot, carrot, potato and water. Cover and simmer for about 45 minutes, until the beetroot is cooked. Add the greens and cook for a further 10 minutes, then add the lemon juice, salt, pepper, paprika and dill.

2 Serve hot, topped with a spoonful of soured cream, soya cream or yoghurt and garnished with chopped parsley.

• **Beetroot Soup with Tomatoes:** Add 175g (6oz) chopped tomatoes and 1 cinnamon stick with the greens. Omit the paprika and dill. Garnish with mint instead of parsley.
• **Cold Summer Borscht:** Prepare the soup ahead of time. Remove the bay leaf. Season, adding double the amount of lemon juice. Blend to a purée and chill. Spoon into individual bowls and serve with a spoonful of yoghurt, soured cream or soya cream on the top.

Golden Cauliflower Soup
If you have ever had the good fortune to stay at the Sivananda Ashram in Kerala, South India, the wonderful combination of cumin, turmeric and coconut will evoke memories of that happy time. This is a superb recipe if you are planning an Indian-style meal. Be careful to not overcook the cumin: the delicate flavour can be easily lost if roasted for too long. Serves 4-6

1 cauliflower
15g (½oz) butter or margarine
1 tablespoon cumin seeds
½ teaspoon turmeric
2 or 3 potatoes, peeled and roughly chopped

1 litre (1¾ pints) water
1 tablespoon desiccated coconut, soaked in enough hot water to cover
salt and pepper

1 Break the cauliflower into small florets, chop the stalk and set aside. Heat the butter or margarine in a large pan, add the cumin seeds and roast for 1 minute, or until you smell the aroma. Lower the heat, add the cauliflower and turmeric and sauté for 5 minutes, stirring well to make sure the florets are coated with turmeric. Remove half of the florets with a slotted spoon and set aside.

2 Add the potatoes and water to the pan and simmer for 15 minutes. Cool slightly, then purée the soup in a food processor or blender until smooth. Return it to the pan and stir in the coconut and its soaking water. Add the reserved cauliflower florets and simmer for another 5 minutes. Season to taste with salt and pepper and serve at once.

Celeriac and Cashew Soup

This makes a lovely winter soup, perfect for festive meals such as Thanksgiving and Christmas. Serves 6-8

15g (½oz) butter or margarine
450g (1lb) celeriac, chopped
4 sticks of celery
100g (4oz) cashew nuts
1 litre (1¾ pints) water

1 potato, chopped
500ml (18fl oz) soya milk
salt and pepper to taste
roasted cashew nuts and parsley sprigs, to garnish

1 Melt the butter or margarine in a heavy pan and sauté the celeriac, celery and nuts over a medium heat until they are slightly browned.

2 Add the water and potato, cover and cook over medium heat for 25 minutes until all the vegetables are tender.

3 Add the soya milk and purée in a food processor or blender. Season with salt and pepper. Return the soup to the pan and heat gently until warm. Serve at once, garnished with roasted cashew nuts and parsley sprigs.

Vichyssoise

Among foods, potatoes are well known for their grounding energy; among asanas, it is the balancing exercises (crow, peacock, tree) that have that distinction. Traditionally served cold as a delightful summer soup, this version can also be heated (be careful that milk or soya milk is not boiled) with no loss of flavour. Serves 6

450g (1lb) potatoes, peeled and diced
200g (7oz) turnips, diced
1 stick of celery, chopped
25g (1oz) butter or 2 tablespoons oil
500ml (18fl oz) water

400ml (14fl oz) milk or soya milk, plus extra if necessary
3-4 tablespoons finely chopped fresh parsley
½ teaspoon salt
pepper to taste

1 Put the potatoes, turnips and celery in a large pan with the butter or oil and the water, adding a little more water if necessary to cover the vegetables. Cover the pan and simmer the vegetables for 15-20 minutes, until they are soft.

2 Transfer the vegetables and the cooking water to a food processor or blender, add the 400ml (14fl oz) milk or soya milk and purée until smooth.

3 Pour the soup into a large bowl and add more soya milk if necessary to bring the soup to the consistency you desire. Stir in the parsley and season with the salt and pepper. Chill for at least 1 hour before serving.

• **Vichyssoise with Cheese:** Substitute 50g (2oz) grated cheese or 25g (1oz) nutritional yeast flakes for some of the milk or soya milk. Serve hot, garnished with a little paprika.

• **Potage Cressonière:** After puréeing the soup, return it to the pan and add 150g (5oz) finely chopped watercress. Add ¼ teaspoon freshly grated nutmeg, if desired. Simmer for about 5 minutes, then stir in the soya milk. Alternatively, use spinach or young spring greens instead of the watercress. If using spring greens, use paprika instead of nutmeg.

Sweetcorn Chowder
This hearty soup is quick and easy to make. Serve with a salad for a winter lunch, or as part of a festive meal. Serves 4-6

4 fresh cobs of corn or 450g (1lb) canned
   sweetcorn kernels
15g (½oz) butter or margarine
250g (9oz) celery or cabbage, chopped

3 potatoes, chopped
500ml (18fl oz) soya milk
1 teaspoon salt
pepper

1 If using fresh corn, scrape off the kernels with a sharp knife.

2 Heat the butter or margarine in a large pan and sauté the celery or cabbage over a medium heat for 5 minutes. Add the potatoes and fresh or canned sweetcorn kernels and cover with water. (You can add the cobs to the liquid while cooking to improve the flavour of the stock.) Half cover the pan and simmer until the corn is tender.

3 Transfer the soup to a food processor or blender, discarding the cobs if they have been added for flavouring, and blend to a coarse purée (the sweetcorn kernel skins will not blend to a smooth purée). Return the soup to the pan and add the soya milk and salt and pepper to taste. Reheat and serve at once.

• **Mexican Corn Chowder:** This chunky variation is a meal in itself. Replace the celery or cabbage with 1 red and 1 green pepper, cored, seeded and chopped. Add 1 teaspoon ground cumin, 2 teaspoons dried oregano and ¼ teaspoon cayenne pepper to the vegetables. Do not blend the soup and omit the soya milk. Serve hot, garnished with coriander leaves. If liked, top each serving with diced vegetarian Cheddar cheese.

Cuban Black Bean Soup
Not to be confused with black-eyed beans, black beans are small, matt black beans, warming by nature and believed to help strengthen kidney energy. In this traditional Cuban recipe, their strong earthy flavour is perfectly complemented by the sweetness of the potatoes and the heat of the ginger. For a more substantial dish, serve with cooked brown rice, either stirred into the soup or served separately. To add extra colour, garnish with strips of blanched sweet potato and parsley sprigs. Serves 4-6

250g (9oz) dried black beans, soaked for
   3-4 hours
1 litre (1¾ pints) water
1 sweet potato or yam, diced
1 bay leaf

1 tablespoon chopped fresh root ginger (optional)
25g (1oz) butter or margarine
salt
yoghurt, fromage frais or grated cheese,
   to serve (optional)

1 Drain the beans and place them in a large pan with the water. Bring to the boil and boil vigorously for 10 minutes. Lower the heat.

2 Add the sweet potato or yam, bay leaf and ginger, if using. Cover and simmer for about 1 hour, or until the beans are tender, adding more water if necessary. Allow to cool slightly, then purée in a food processor or blender until the mixture is smooth (leave a few beans whole to stir into the purée, if preferred).

3 Return the purée to the pan and add the butter or margarine. Season to taste with salt. Simmer for 10 minutes. Serve at once, topped with yoghurt, fromage frais or grated cheese, if desired.

Lentil Soup
Rich in protein and iron, lentils are used in everything from light summery soups to hearty winter dishes. They do not need to be soaked, but soaking them for 30 minutes helps to remove the phytates that might impede the absorption of iron. Serves 6

1-2 tablespoons oil, butter or ghee	2 bay leaves
2 carrots, diced	1 tablespoon tomato purée (optional)
1 medium swede or turnip, diced	1.5 litres (2¾ pints) hot water
2 sticks of celery, chopped	1 teaspoon salt or 1 tablespoon tamari
400g (14oz) lentils, soaked for 30 minutes	1 teaspoon each dried oregano and thyme

1 Heat the oil, butter or ghee in a heavy-based pan and sauté the carrots, swede or turnip and celery for 3-4 minutes. Drain the lentils and add them to the pan with the bay leaves, tomato purée, if using, and 1 litre (1¾ pints) of the water. Bring to the boil, then reduce the heat, half cover and simmer for 15-20 minutes, or until the lentils are soft.

2 Add the salt or tamari, oregano, thyme and as much of the remaining water as is necessary to achieve the consistency of your choice. Simmer for 2-3 minutes and serve.

Split Pea Soup
This recipe is a winter favourite at the Sivananda Headquarters in Quebec, where temperatures often drop to -40°C/-40°F. Serves 8

225g (8oz) split peas (yellow or green)	1 teaspoon dried basil
1.5 litres (2¾ pints) water	½ teaspoon ground ginger
2 tablespoons oil, butter or margarine	1 teaspoon ground cumin
2 carrots, sliced into thin rounds	1 teaspoon honey (optional)
2 sticks of celery, finely chopped	1 tablespoon lemon juice (optional)
2 potatoes, cut into large cubes	1 teaspoon salt and ¼ teaspoon pepper

1 Wash the split peas and place them in a large pan with the water. Cover and simmer for about 40 minutes, until tender.

2 Heat the oil, butter or margarine in a separate pan and sauté the vegetables with the herbs and spices over a medium heat for 5 minutes. Add them to the cooked split peas. Bring back to the boil and simmer, covered, for a further 20 minutes, until the peas are very soft. Add the honey and lemon juice, if using. Season with the salt and pepper and serve at once.

Tofu Vegetable Soup Orientale
A simple, delicate soup, ideal if you want a light, but flavourful course before heavier dishes. Serves 4-6

1 tablespoon oil	250g (9oz) tofu, cut into bite-sized pieces
50g (2oz) water chestnuts, sliced	1.5 litres (2¾ pints) boiling water
50g (2oz) bamboo shoots, sliced	75g (3oz) mange-tout, trimmed and sliced
75g (3oz) kohlrabi, chopped	50ml (2fl oz) tamari

1 Heat the oil in a large pan, add the water chestnuts, bamboo shoots, kohlrabi and tofu. Stir-fry for about 4 minutes.

2 Add the boiling water and simmer for 10 minutes. Add the mange-tout and simmer for another 2-3 minutes. Season with tamari and serve at once.

Miso A salty paste made from beans and/or grains, miso is mostly used to add flavour to soups and sauces. It is highly beneficial in the diet as a source of protein and is reputed to have remarkable medicinal properties. In Japan it is used to cure colds, improve metabolism, clear the skin, and help develop resistance to parasitic diseases! Each type of miso adds a different flavour to food. It is best to buy organic miso at your local health food store – you use so little, it is worth the expense. Light miso is fragrant and sweet. Red-brown miso is aromatic and tasty, and dark miso is pungent and salty. Never boil miso as it destroys the helpful micro-organisms. Also, do not reheat miso soup as it destroys the nutritional value.

Miso Soup
Miso soup is warm and soothing on a cold day; refreshing on a hot day. This basic soup can be varied by adding grains or noodles. Serves 6

a few pieces of arame or wakame seaweed, soaked in enough water to cover for 5 minutes
2 teaspoons sesame oil
175g (6oz) finely chopped or sliced vegetables (cabbage, celery, carrots, swede, turnip)

2 teaspoons grated fresh root ginger
1 litre (1³/₄ pints) water
4 tablespoons dark miso
2 tablespoons fresh parsley or coriander leaves

1 Drain the arame or wakame and cut into 2.5cm (1in) strips; set aside. Heat the oil in a wok or heavy pan. Add the vegetables and ginger, and sauté for about 5 minutes.

2 Add the seaweed and water and bring to the boil. Half cover and simmer for 15 minutes. Remove from the heat. Mix the miso with a little of the soup, then stir it into the pan. Serve at once, garnished with parsley or coriander.

Salmoreio
Elizabeth, the mother of one of our staff, contributed this recipe; it joined our repertory during one of our month-long yoga teachers' training courses in Spain. Prana-laden ripe tomatoes bring out the true character of this traditional chilled Andalusian soup. The amount of tomato juice depends on how thick you like the soup. Serve with fresh bread, rice cakes or crudités. Serves 4-6

450g (1lb) ripe tomatoes, chopped
2 tablespoons chopped fresh basil
50g (2oz) fresh breadcrumbs
3 tablespoons extra virgin olive oil
2 tablespoons lemon juice
1 tablespoon tomato purée

1 teaspoon chopped fresh root ginger
½ teaspoon cayenne pepper
1 teaspoon salt
pepper to taste
125-250ml (4-8fl oz) tomato juice or water

Put all the ingredients in a food processor or blender, adding 125ml (4fl oz) tomato juice or water. Blend until thick and smooth. Add the remaining tomato juice or water if the soup is too thick. Chill before serving.

• **Gazpacho:** Omit the ginger and half the breadcrumbs. Add ½ a peeled and chopped cucumber, ½ a cored, seeded and chopped green pepper, 1 chopped stick of celery, and 2 tablespoons finely chopped parsley. Use tomato juice rather than water. Blend and chill. To serve, add some ice cubes and garnish with chopped cucumber and pepper and/or wholewheat croûtons.

GLORIOUS GRAINS

*"Like grain, the mortal decays
And like grain, he is born again."*

Katha Upanishad, I. 6

"Many people consider life as a straight line, from A to B, from birth to death. But yoga masters speak of a triangle. The first point represents birth; the line going upwards represents growth. The top point represents youth; then the downward line is decay or old age, and at the end of decay is the last point, representing death. The bottom line represents life hereafter which leads us again to the first point, birth – reincarnation. Again there is growth; again youth, decay, death, and life hereafter, and then again birth. So life goes on and on and on, forever and ever and ever."

Swami Vishnu-devananda

The yogic diet is essentially grain-based. Whole grains are the primary source of carbohydrates, the origin of energy for the human body. Complex carbohydrates are abundant in nature, relatively inexpensive and filling. Unrefined grains are rich in fibre and B vitamins and supply about half of the amino acids that form protein. They should be eaten every day, preferably with foods containing complementary proteins, such as pulses. Most of the world's population survives on a diet of pulse and grain combinations.

Weigh or measure grains, then rinse them two or three times, until the water runs clear. Drain and put into a heavy saucepan, together with the appropriate amount of water (see chart below). Bring to the boil, reduce the heat and simmer until all the water has been absorbed.

Grains may be pre-soaked to reduce the cooking time. Alternatively, they may be dry roasted in the oven at 190°C/375°F/Gas mark 5 for 15-30 minutes, or in a heated dry frying pan over a high heat for a few minutes, before boiling, to give them a sweet, nutty flavour.

COOKING GRAINS

The volume of water needed for cooking varies from twice to four and a half times the volume of the grain.

Grain	Amount	Volume of water	Cooking time	Serves
Barley	200g (7oz)	2½ times	35-40 minutes	4-6
Buckwheat	200g (7oz)	Twice	15-25 minutes	4-6
Bulgar	200g (7oz)	Twice	Pour boiling water over and leave for 15-20 minutes	4-6
Cornmeal	200g (7oz)	3-3½ times	15 minutes	4-6
Couscous	200g (7oz)	Twice	Pour boiling water over, cover and leave 15-20 minutes	4-6
Millet	200g (7oz)	2½-3 times	30-45 minutes	4-6
Oat flakes	100g (4oz)	2½-3 times	15-30 minutes	2-3
Quinoa	200g (7oz)	Twice	15 minutes	4
Rice, basmati	200g (7oz)	Twice	20-35 minutes	4-6
Rice, brown	200g (7oz)	2-2½ times	40-50 minutes	4
Rye grains	200g (7oz)	3½ times	2 hours	4
Wheat grains	200g (7oz)	4½ times	45-60 minutes	4-6

Rice One of the great staples of the world, rice features heavily in the yogic diet. In Asia, rice is the emblem of prosperity (both material and spiritual), happiness and nourishment. In India, rice is sacred and is used in all rituals. When guests arrive they are asked "Have you had your rice?", as the first duty to the guest is to offer him/her food. Rice has a balancing effect on the entire digestive system and soothes the nervous system. Because it is neither heating nor cooling to the system, rice can be combined with herbs and spices in a myriad of ways to harmonize imbalances in the body. Short grain brown rice offers the richest source of vitamins and minerals. Most popular in Ayurveda, basmati rice is a light and aromatic long-grain variety with a cooling effect on the body. It is good for calming an irritated gut and is easier to digest than brown rice.

To cook brown rice, rinse the rice first, then cook in a heavy-based saucepan with a tight fitting lid. The general rule is one measure of rice to two or two and a half measures of cold water. Bring to the boil, then reduce the heat, cover the pan and simmer gently for 40-50 minutes. Do not remove the lid during this time as the steam plays an essential part in the cooking process. After about 45 minutes the water will have been absorbed and the rice will be tender with a delicious chewy texture. Another way to cook rice is to gently toast it in a dry pan for a few minutes, then add the water and cook as above.

To cook basmati rice, gently wash it in cold water to remove much of the starch, changing the water until the water is clear. Bring just under twice the volume of water to rice to the boil, add the rice and a pinch of salt to taste, reduce the heat, cover and cook for 10-15 minutes by which time all the water should be absorbed. Remove from the heat and allow to stand for 5 minutes before removing the lid.

Rice Pilau
Basmati is the rice considered to be the best among the many Indian varieties – its name means 'queen of fragrance' – and is the one most often used in festive Indian dishes. Brown basmati rice contains more nutrients than the white variety. Rice pilau can be used along with dal to make a simple meal, or can be used as part of a more elaborate meal. Serves 4-6

300g (10oz) basmati rice
50ml (2fl oz) ghee or vegetable oil
50g (2oz) raw cashews, almonds or pistachio nuts, chopped
1 teaspoon cumin seeds
2cm (3/4in) piece of fresh root ginger, peeled and shredded

1-2 green chillies, seeded and finely chopped
600ml (1 pint) hot water
150g (5oz) fresh peas or finely sliced green beans
½ teaspoon garam masala
1 teaspoon salt
50g (2oz) raisins (optional)

1 Wash the rice and soak in cold water for 15-20 minutes, then drain. Heat the ghee or oil in a heavy pan over a low heat. Add the nuts and sauté, stirring constantly until golden brown. Remove from the oil.

2 Increase the heat to medium, add the cumin seeds, ginger and chillies to the pan and cook until the cumin is golden brown, stirring constantly. Pour in the rice and stir-fry for 2 minutes. Add the hot water, peas, garam masala, salt and raisins, if using. Bring to the boil, then reduce the heat to very low, cover with a tight fitting lid and cook gently for 10-15 minutes, until all the water is absorbed and the rice is tender and fluffy. Serve at once.

Rice Salad

Poornima, the full moon night, is considered by yogis to be especially auspicious for spiritual practice. Guru Poornima, the full moon around mid-July, is dedicated to the teacher. It is the occasion of the London Centre's annual boat trip on the River Thames, complete with chanting and a feast. This recipe, which may be prepared in advance, is usually one of the highlights of the celebration. It is served along with other salads (pages 96-99) and items from the Middle Eastern Feast (page 142). Serves 8

300g (10oz) brown or basmati rice
600ml (1 pint) water
75ml (3fl oz) olive oil
3 tablespoons lemon juice
2 tablespoons chopped fresh herbs, such as
 parsley, basil, mint, lemon balm

450g (1lb) mixed vegetables, such as blanched
 asparagus or peas, avocado, sweet pepper,
 carrot, celery, cucumber, fennel, stoned olives,
 diced where necessary
1 teaspoon salt
¼ teaspoon pepper

1 Place the rice in a heavy pan with the water. Bring to the boil, cover and simmer for 35-40 minutes for brown rice or about 20-35 minutes for basmati rice, until all the water is absorbed.

2 Allow the rice to cool, then toss the cooked rice, olive oil and lemon juice gently with a fork (a spoon tends to mash the rice). Mix in the herbs and diced vegetables. Season with the salt and pepper.

3 Rice salad can be served right away, but it tastes better if the flavours are allowed to blend for about 2 hours. Serve each portion on a lettuce leaf or in a hollowed-out tomato or pepper. Alternatively, press into a lightly oiled mould and chill in the refrigerator for several hours before turning out.

• **Seeded Rice Salad:** Replace the vegetables and herbs with 2 teaspoons sesame seeds, 2 tablespoons sunflower seeds and 2 tablespoons pumpkin seeds toasted separately. Substitute 3 tablespoons tahini for the olive oil.

Congee

Yogis have traditionally eaten this rice soup for thousands of years, as it is easy to prepare, nutritious and tastes good. It is the favourite evening meal at our Sivananda Yoga Vedanta Nataraja Centre in New Delhi, especially in winter time. A popular breakfast or supper dish throughout Asia, congee (also known as kanji) is a very calming food that soothes and strengthens the digestion, and for this reason it is often given to invalids or children. Serves 4-6

200g (7oz) brown rice
2.5cm (1in) piece fresh root ginger, peeled and
 sliced or chopped

3 litres (5¼ pints) water
salt, tamari or Gomasio (page 118) to taste,
 or nori, toasted and crumbled

1 Place the rice and ginger in a heavy pan with the water. Bring to the boil, cover and cook over a medium heat for about 1 hour, until the rice breaks down to a soupy consistency. Remove the pan from the heat and spoon the soup into individual bowls.

2 Season to taste with salt, tamari or gomasio, or sprinkle toasted and crumbled nori over the top, and serve at once.

Stir-fried Rice with Bean Sprouts *The ever-*
popular Chinese stir-fry is fast, easy and a full meal in itself. Serves 4-6

3 tablespoons oil
2 teaspoons grated or chopped fresh root ginger
1 red pepper, cored, seeded and coarsely
 chopped
175g (6oz) bean sprouts (either mung or soya)
200g (7oz) cabbage, shredded
200g (7oz) water chestnuts, sliced

200g (7oz) bamboo shoots, sliced
100g (4oz) baby corn
100g (4oz) mange-tout, sliced into 2.5cm (1in)
 lengths
250g (9oz) firm tofu, cubed or broken
350g (12oz) cooked rice
tamari

1 Heat the oil in a wok or heavy frying pan and stir-fry the ginger for about 1 minute. Add the chopped pepper and stir-fry for 2 minutes.

2 Add the other vegetables and the tofu and cook for 2 minutes. Stir in the cooked rice and mix well. Remove from the heat and add tamari to taste. Serve at once.

Paella *The traditional Spanish dish, is given a yogic 'twist' by using brown rice*
and arame, one of the milder tasting sea vegetables. Like all sea vegetables, arame
has a cooling effect and helps to cleanse the body of toxins. It is important to soak sea
vegetables in water to remove the excess salt before using. This paella makes a
delicious meal served with a green salad. Serves 6

300g (10oz) brown rice
600ml (1 pint) water
300g (10oz) firm tofu, cut into cubes
50ml (2fl oz) tamari
2 tablespoons arame seaweed, soaked in enough
 water to cover for about 5 minutes
oil for deep-frying
1 aubergine, halved lengthwise and thinly sliced

2 tablespoons olive oil
2 carrots, sliced diagonally
1 red pepper, cored, seeded and cut into strips
1 teaspoon turmeric
3-4 tablespoons lemon juice
24 stoned black olives
2 tablespoons chopped fresh parsley

1 Put the brown rice in a heavy pan and add the water. Bring to the boil, lower the heat, cover and simmer for 35-40 minutes, until all the water is absorbed and the rice is tender.

2 Meanwhile, marinate the tofu in the tamari for 30 minutes, then drain. Drain the arame.

3 Heat the oil for frying in a heavy frying pan. Add the aubergine slices and tofu cubes, a few at a time, and cook until sealed and crispy. Drain on paper towels.

4 Heat the olive oil in the frying pan. Add the carrots, red pepper and turmeric and sauté until the vegetables are tender. Stir in the cooked rice and lemon juice. Gently fold in the tofu cubes, aubergine and arame. Garnish with the black olives and chopped parsley and serve hot.

Baked Rice

Sankar and Tejas, our 'men in Toronto', sent in this recipe along with the following comments: "This is a grain recipe we have made quite a few times. We really like it because it is simple, tasty and the rice is very well cooked, so it's much easier to digest. It's great with stir-fry veggies. Good cooking!!!" Serves 4-6

3 teaspoons hijiki seaweed, soaked in enough
  water to cover for 15 minutes
100g (4oz) raw cashew nuts, chopped
1 tablespoon oil
2 carrots, cut into matchsticks
200g (7oz) cabbage, finely shredded

100g (4oz) aubergine, cubed
250g (9oz) brown rice
100g (4oz) red lentils
750ml (1¼ pints) water
100g (4oz) fresh peas or green beans, sliced
1 teaspoon salt

1 Drain the hijiki. Roast the cashew nuts in a hot dry frying pan until browned. Remove from the pan and set aside. Heat the oil in a large pan and sauté the carrots, cabbage and aubergine over a medium heat for 5-7 minutes, until softened slightly. Stir in the rice and sauté for 1 minute. Add the hijiki and sauté lightly for a few moments. Add the lentils and water. Bring to the boil, lower the heat, cover tightly and cook over a low heat for about 30 minutes.

2 Meanwhile, preheat the oven to 180°C/350°F/Gas mark 4. Uncover the pan and, if necessary, add another 50-125ml (2-4fl oz) water along with the peas or beans, salt and cashews. Transfer to a greased casserole dish, cover and bake in the oven for about 20 minutes. Serve hot.

Quinoa Quinoa (pronounced keen-wa) is an ancient grain that is making a come-back. It has a high amino acid content, is easy to cook and digest, and is gluten-free, making it a great alternative for people with corn or wheat allergies. It can be substituted for rice or millet in most recipes. Quinoa must be washed thoroughly; place in a fine mesh sieve and rinse until the water runs clear.

Aubergine Quinoa Roast

This high-energy grain from South America's Andes mountains is given an international flavour in this vegetable-rich dish, needing only a green salad to complement it. Serves 4

4 tablespoons sesame oil
350g (12oz) aubergine, cut into 8 thick slices
2 tablespoons tamari
50ml (2fl oz) lemon juice
125ml (4fl oz) water

1 teaspoon grated fresh root ginger
200g (7oz) quinoa, washed
1 large red pepper, cored, seeded and sliced
2 courgettes, coarsely grated
parsley sprigs, to garnish

1 Preheat the oven to 180°C/350°F/Gas mark 4. Heat the sesame oil in a frying pan and cook the aubergine slices until browned. Arrange them in a single layer in a baking dish. Combine the tamari, lemon juice, water and ginger and pour over the aubergine slices. Bake in the oven for 10 minutes. Turn the slices over and cook for 10 minutes, until most of the liquid has been absorbed.

2 Place the quinoa in a large pan with double its volume of water. Bring to the boil, cover and simmer for 15 minutes, until tender. Drain if necessary. Add the red pepper and courgettes to the sesame oil remaining in the frying pan and sauté until soft. Add the quinoa, mix well and spoon over the aubergine. Press down well. Return to the oven and cook for 5-10 minutes. Serve hot, garnished with parsley sprigs.

Wheat Rich in vitamins and minerals, whole wheat is an essential ingredient in a yogi's diet, eaten as a grain, made into pasta or used as flour for bread. It is important to avoid refined wheat as most of the energy-giving nutrients of the grain have been removed. Wheat has a cooling effect on the system and can help to reduce inflammation. It also stimulates the liver to cleanse itself. Wheat allergies are very common, but usually they are an allergic reaction to the quantity and quality of the processed wheat that most of us eat; organically grown whole wheat is less likely to cause a reaction. Gluten is a protein in wheat flour which traps air in the dough and makes bread rise. It is also found in rye and barley, but in smaller quantities. If you find that wheat, or these other grains, cause bloating, gas, stomach pain, indigestion or excessive mucus, they are best avoided, especially during pregnancy. Rice, millet, quinoa or spelt may be substituted. Most people with wheat sensitivities find that they can easily tolerate rye and barley – and that organically grown wheat does not disturb them.

Spelt is an ancient relative of wheat that is enjoying a renewed popularity. Spelt can usually be tolerated by people with wheat and gluten sensitivities. Higher in protein and fibre than most varieties of wheat, spelt is available in health food stores in the form of pastas, flour, breads and whole grains. It may be substituted for wheat in any recipe, using the same quantities.

Wholewheat Bread
Our daily bread, more than any other food, symbolizes the giving of human, as well as divine, love. Eating bread can be a mystical as well as communal experience. Fresh bread that has been baked with love has the mysterious power of bringing warmth and togetherness into any home or gathering. God is everywhere, but the daily ritual of the breaking of bread can serve to bring that awareness to mind. Chew the bread well and think of the many blessings that you have. Many people in the world have neither enough food to eat nor clean water to drink. They do not have a healthy body to enable them to work out their karma. In the words of Swami Sivananda: "The first wealth is health. It is the greatest of all possessions. It is the basis of all virtues. The person with health has hope, and he who has hope has everything." Makes 2 loaves, about 900g (2lb) each

2 tablespoons dried yeast
900ml (1½ pints) tepid water
50ml (2fl oz) oil

3 tablespoons barley malt syrup
1.5kg (3lb 5oz) wholewheat flour
2 teaspoons sea salt

1 Sprinkle the yeast into the water in a bowl and leave in a warm place for 10 minutes. Add the oil, barley malt syrup and half the flour and blend well. Cover and leave to rise for 30 minutes.

2 Stir in the rest of the flour and salt and knead to a smooth dough, adding a little more flour if necessary (the dough should not be too sticky). Leave to rise again for 45-60 minutes, until doubled in size.

3 Punch down the risen dough to knock out any large air bubbles, shape into two loaves and place in two lightly oiled 900g (2lb) loaf tins. Leave to prove until the top of the centre of the dough is level with the top of the tins. Do not let it over rise or the dough will crack. Meanwhile, preheat the oven to 230°C/450°F/Gas mark 8. Bake in the oven on the top shelf for 15 minutes. Reduce the heat to 190°C/375°F/Gas mark 5 and bake for a further 1 hour. Leave to cool before serving – hot bread tastes great but it is hard to digest.

- **Poppy Seed Bread:** Add to the basic mix 50g (2oz) poppy seeds, 1 teaspoon almond essence, 1 tablespoon raisins or chopped dates.
- **Seed Bread:** Add 2 tablespoons each of poppy seeds, sesame seeds, sunflower seeds and pumpkin seeds with the flour.
- **Sesame Honey Bread:** Use sesame oil in the basic mix and add 100g (4oz) sesame seeds and 1-2 tablespoons honey.
- **Oat Bread:** Reduce the amount of wholewheat flour to 1.3kg (2lb 14oz). Add 200g (7oz) rolled oats or 75g (3oz) cornmeal and 100g (4oz) rolled oats.
- **Rye Bread:** Reduce the amount of wholewheat flour to 750g (1lb 10oz) and add 750g (1lb 10oz) rye flour and 1 tablespoon crushed caraway seeds.

Chapatis

This is the basic flat bread that is served throughout northern India, always cooked fresh for each meal. One of the great delights of Sivananda Kutir, our small Himalayan ashram, is to sit on the kitchen veranda and be served hot, freshly made chapatis. Just in front, the Ganges River roars by; overhead, the eagles soar. Chapatis are the staple food of North India, as rice is in the south. They are the 'spoon' of the meal. To eat, break off a piece of chapati (with the right hand) and use it to scoop up vegetables, dal, pickle and yoghurt or raita. Makes about 18

250g (9oz) wholewheat flour
1 teaspoon salt

about 175ml (6fl oz) water
ghee or oil for brushing (optional)

1 Combine the flour and salt in a bowl. Gradually mix in the water until the dough binds together, but is not sticky or wet. Knead well for about 10 minutes, until firm and elastic. Oil a bowl, turn the dough in it twice, then cover with a damp tea-towel. Leave to sit for 1 hour, then knead again.

2 Form the dough into 1cm (½in) diameter balls. Flatten them and roll into discs about 3mm (⅛in) thick, using an oiled rolling pin. As you do this, roll the chapati a couple of times and turn it slightly; repeat the turning as you roll to prevent the chapati sticking to the board. Make sure each chapati is symmetrical so that it puffs up well.

3 Cook in a very hot ungreased pan over a high heat for a few seconds on each side, until slightly brown. Using a damp cloth, press on each side to make the bread puff up in the centre. Brush the chapatis lightly with ghee or oil, if desired, and pile them up as you make them, wrapping them in a slightly damp cloth until ready to serve.

- **Puris:** Deep-fry the chapatis in hot oil, pressing down once with the back of a large, metal spoon to puff them up. These are better than chapatis for a feast, as they can be cooked in advance.
- **Paratha:** Follow the chapati recipe. Roll out the dough, making sure it is symmetrical. Brush the top with melted ghee; dust with flour. Pleat the edges until a fist-size parcel has been formed. Flatten; roll out again. Turn it over and do the same on the other side. The more times you do this, the flakier the paratha will be – twice is the minimum. Cook on a very hot ungreased pan for a few seconds, brush with a little ghee and flip it over. Repeat on the other side. It is ready when lightly brown. Parathas may be stuffed with any curried vegetable: served with yoghurt they are a typical breakfast or evening meal in northern India.

Banana Bread

Half cake, half bread, but doubly good – even better spread with butter – is the unanimous verdict of the London Sivanada Yoga Centre. Banana breads tend to be moist, so they must be cooked in well regulated ovens, otherwise the outside will be overcooked before the inside is ready. If you have this problem, get your oven checked or try baking at a lower temperature. Makes 1 loaf

3 very ripe bananas
100g (4oz) clear honey
200g (7oz) wholewheat flour
½ teaspoon salt

1 teaspoon bicarbonate of soda
2 tablespoons melted butter or oil
75g (3oz) nuts, chopped (optional)

1 Preheat the oven to 180°C/350°F/Gas mark 4. Purée the bananas in a food processor or blender or mash them with a fork. Add the honey and blend again or mix with a whisk. Sift the flour, salt and bicarbonate of soda together. Add the flour to the honey and banana mixture and stir with a whisk to combine everything. Add the butter or oil and the nuts, if using.

2 Pour into a 23 x 12.5cm (9 x 5in) greased loaf tin and bake in the oven for about 1 hour. To check that it is cooked, press lightly with a finger to see if the bread pops up, or insert a cocktail stick into the centre to see if it comes out clean. Cool on a wire rack.

Peaceful Pizza

This recipe comes from Ganesha, our Yogi of the North. He is probably the best vegetarian pizza maker, and definitely the best yoga teacher, in Scotland. If you have a wheat allergy, substitute spelt flour for the wheat flour. The variety of toppings is infinite. Serves 4-8

Base:
350g (12oz) strong white bread flour
4g easy-bake dried yeast
1 tablespoon olive oil
2 teaspoons demerara sugar
½ teaspoon sea salt
about 200ml (7fl oz) tepid water

Topping:
1 quantity of Tomato Sauce (page 123)
100g (4oz) vegetarian cheese, grated, or tahini
2 red or yellow peppers (or 1 of each), cored, seeded and sliced (optional)
12 olives (optional)
olive oil for drizzling

1 To make the base, combine all the ingredients, except the water, in a bowl. Gradually add the water, mixing by hand until the dough forms a slightly sticky ball. The exact amount of water will depend on the flour used.

2 Turn the dough out on to a floured board and knead well for about 10 minutes, adding a little more flour if necessary. Alternatively, mix in a food processor until a slightly sticky dough is formed, then turn out and knead for about 1 minute. Put the dough into a lightly oiled mixing bowl, cover with a cloth and leave to rise in a warm place for about 1 hour, or until doubled in size.

3 Preheat the oven to 230°C/450°F/Gas mark 8. Divide the dough in half. Knead each portion into a ball, then roll out to fit two lightly greased 32.5 x 25cm (13 x 10in) baking sheets. Place the dough on the baking sheets. Divide the tomato sauce between the pizzas and spread out evenly. Sprinkle the cheese over the sauce. Decorate with peppers and olives, if using, and a drizzle of olive oil. Bake the pizzas in the oven for about 15 minutes, then swop them over if they are on separate shelves in the oven and cook for 5-10 minutes, until the base is slightly brown.

Wholewheat Spaghetti with Miso Sauce

*An unusual and delicious recipe blending East-West cuisines, but remember that
noodles originated in Asia. For the miso sauce, use red ake miso or dark hatcho miso
(see Glossary, page 156). If possible, make the sauce 6-8 hours in advance to allow
the flavours to blend.* Serves 4-6

2 tablespoons oil
2 sticks of celery, finely chopped
100g (4oz) fennel, chopped
3 tomatoes, diced
3 green peppers, cored, seeded and diced
½ a carrot, grated
400ml (14fl oz) water
4 bay leaves

5 tablespoons miso
15g (½oz) butter or margarine
1 tablespoon chopped fresh basil
pepper to taste
500g (1lb 2oz) wholewheat spaghetti
grated cheese or nutritional yeast
    flakes for sprinkling (optional)

1 Heat the oil in a heavy pan and sauté the celery and fennel over a medium heat for about
10 minutes. Add the tomatoes, green peppers and carrot and sauté for another 15 minutes.

2 Add the water and bay leaves. Bring to the boil and simmer uncovered for 10 minutes. Remove
from the heat and stir in the miso, butter or margarine and basil. Season to taste with pepper.

3 Cook the spaghetti in boiling water until *al dente* (tender but still firm to the bite). Drain well.
Remove the bay leaves from the sauce and stir in the hot spaghetti. Add the cheese or yeast
flakes, if using, and serve at once.

• Add 150-200g (5-7oz) cubed tofu when you add the vegetables.

Vegetarian Lasagne *There are many ways to make lasagne. This
one is a favourite of Swami Mahadevananda, the Italian-born director of the Sivananda
Dhanwanthari Ashram in Kerala, South India. Serve it with a green salad.* Serves 4-6

175g (6oz) spinach, steamed and squeezed dry
250g (9oz) firm tofu, crumbled and drained
salt and pepper
2 tablespoons olive oil
1 red pepper, cored, seeded and cut into
    matchsticks

2 courgettes, cut into matchsticks
1 quantity of Tomato Sauce (page 123)
6 sheets of dried lasagne, cooked and drained
100g (4oz) vegetarian Cheddar cheese, grated
2 tablespoons sunflower or sesame seeds
2 tablespoons nutritional yeast flakes (optional)

1 Preheat the oven to 180°C/350°F/Gas mark 4. Chop the spinach and mix it with the tofu.
Season with salt and pepper. Heat the oil and sauté the pepper and courgette strips over a
medium heat for 3 minutes.

2 Spoon a layer of tomato sauce into an oiled 25 x 20cm (10 x 8in) baking dish. Cover this with a
layer of cooked lasagne, then half the tofu and spinach mixture, and half the courgette and pepper
strips. Sprinkle with half the grated Cheddar cheese.

3 Repeat the layers, then sprinkle the sunflower or sesame seeds and the yeast flakes, if using,
over the top. Bake in the oven for 50-60 minutes, until bubbling and golden. Serve at once.

• Omit the cheese.

Couscous with Spicy Vegetables

Couscous consists of tiny pearls of pasta made from finely milled semolina wheat. It is widely used in North African countries, where it has given its name to this traditional dish served with a delicious vegetable stew. The only accompaniment it needs is a crisp green salad. Bulgar wheat may be substituted for the couscous. Serves 4-6

225g (8oz) chick peas, soaked
1 litre (1¾ pints) cold water
225g (8oz) couscous
400ml (14fl oz) hot water
2 tablespoons olive oil
100g (4oz) chopped white cabbage
1 teaspoon cayenne pepper
1 teaspoon paprika
2 teaspoons yellow mustard seeds
2 potatoes, diced

2 green peppers, cored, seeded and diced
350g (12oz) courgettes, thickly sliced
175g (6oz) okra, sliced
2 carrots, cut into thick slices
350g (12oz) tomatoes, chopped
50g (2oz) raisins (optional)
salt and pepper
2 tablespoons chopped fresh parsley
parsley sprigs, to garnish

1 Drain the chick peas and place in a pan with the cold water. Half cover and cook over a medium heat for 1-1½ hours, until tender. Drain and set aside to cool.

2 Put the couscous into a bowl, cover with the hot water and leave to soak for 15 minutes. Meanwhile, heat the oil in a large pan, over which a steamer will fit. Add the cabbage to the pan and sauté gently until softened. Stir in the spices and cook over a medium heat for 1 minute. Add the potatoes and continue cooking for 3-4 minutes, until they begin to soften. Add the green peppers, courgettes, okra, carrots, tomatoes, cooked chick peas and raisins, if using.

3 Drain the couscous thoroughly and put into a steamer or colander lined with muslin. Fit this over the pan of vegetables, making sure the bottom does not touch the vegetables. Place the lid on and steam the couscous for 20 minutes, stirring the vegetables occasionally until they are tender and the couscous is heated through. Season both the couscous and vegetables with salt and pepper to taste. Add the chopped parsley to the vegetables.

4 Transfer the couscous to a large round serving dish and separate the grains with a fork. Pour the vegetables into a separate dish, or make a well in the mound of couscous and place the vegetables in it. Serve at once, garnished with parsley sprigs.

Barley One of the most ancient grains, barley has remained in the diet of many cultures around the world for a good reason. Its slightly sweet taste and chewy texture combine well with most vegetables and seasonings, especially in soups and casseroles. It is a highly nutritious food, rich in iron, calcium, potassium, B vitamins and protein, as well as fibre. It has a cooling, anti-inflammatory effect on the body. Traditionally, barley water was fed to convalescents and used in cooling summer drinks. It is important to buy pot barley, not the pearl barley available in supermarkets as this has had the nutritious hull and bran layers removed. It is easy to cook using the same method as brown rice (see chart on page 46). It is especially tasty and healthy when pre-roasted; a very acid-forming grain, barley has an alkaline effect on the body when roasted. Roasted barley can be ground and sprinkled on cereals or used as a coffee substitute. Barley is also very good sprouted (when it is known as barley grass), providing a rich source of chlorophyll, beta-carotene and minerals.

Creole Barley
This is barley with a bite, proving the point that you do not need to spend a lot of money for well-balanced yet tasty food. Serves 6

1 tablespoon olive oil
2½ teaspoons cumin seeds
1 large red pepper, cored, seeded and diced
2 sticks of celery, diced
¼ teaspoon crushed dried chillies
2 teaspoons dried oregano

3 tomatoes, diced
300g (10oz) pot barley, washed
900ml (1½ pints) water
1 teaspoon salt
1-2 tablespoons chopped fresh coriander

1 Heat the oil in a heavy pan and sauté the cumin seeds over a high heat for a few seconds, taking care not to burn them, then add the red pepper, celery, dried chillies and oregano and stir-fry for 2 minutes.

2 Add the diced tomatoes, barley, water and salt. Bring to the boil, half cover and simmer for 35-40 minutes, until the barley is tender and the liquid has been absorbed. Add the chopped coriander and serve at once.

Barley with Tomatoes, Olives and Dill
This is a very elegant way of using barley, a hearty grain. Served with Ratatouille (page 89), this makes a delicious Mediterranean-style meal. An interesting variation is to omit the oil and dry roast the barley until it becomes aromatic, then add the water. This gives the dish a slightly smoky taste, and a more drying effect on the body. Serves 4-6

1 tablespoon oil
225g (8oz) pot barley, washed
600ml (1 pint) boiling water
500g (1 lb 2oz) tomatoes, chopped
50g (2oz) black olives, stoned and finely
   chopped

2 teaspoons dried dill weed
150ml (5fl oz) crème fraîche or fromage frais
salt and pepper to taste
100g (4oz) vegetarian Cheddar cheese, grated
100g (4oz) tomatoes, sliced

1 Heat the oil in a large pan and sauté the barley for 3-4 minutes. Add the boiling water and cook for 35-40 minutes, until tender. Meanwhile, preheat the oven to 190°C/375°F/Gas mark 5.

2 Drain the barley. Combine all the ingredients, except for half the grated cheese and the sliced tomatoes, and spoon into a baking dish. Top with the remaining cheese and tomato slices.

3 Bake in the oven for 10-15 minutes, until the cheese has melted and is beginning to brown. Serve at once.

• For a vegan version, use 200g (7oz) tofu instead of the crème fraîche or fromage frais. Sprinkle with nutritional yeast flakes instead of Cheddar cheese or omit entirely.
• For a vegetable-rich dish, sauté a selection of chopped vegetables such as celery, red and green peppers, carrots and courgettes in a little butter or oil until soft and add to the mixture before baking.

Oats Renowned for their warming properties and used as a staple food in many cold climate cultures of the world, oats are high in fibre and rich in vitamins E and B and the minerals calcium, potassium and magnesium. They increase general vitality and are beneficial to the nervous system, helping to relieve stress and tension. Their high silicon content makes them desirable for healthy arterial walls and the renewal of all connective tissues. They are soothing to stomach and intestinal walls, and help to lower cholesterol. Oats make a good thickening agent in soups, gravies, sauces and stews. Rolled oats are commonly available in health food stores and are preferable to the quick cooking variety available in supermarkets.

East-West Hot Pot
This crunchy hot pot makes an unusual lunch dish, and shows just how versatile oats are. Serves 4-6

1 tablespoon oil
100g (4oz) rolled oats
50g (2oz) raw peanuts
100g (4oz) peas or sliced green beans
100g (4oz) carrots, chopped
½ teaspoon cayenne pepper or 4-5 green
  chillies, seeded and chopped

1 small tomato, chopped
1 teaspoon salt
400ml (14fl oz) boiling water
1 tablespoon grated vegetarian cheese (optional)
15g (½oz) butter or margarine
Coconut or Mint Chutney (page 125), to serve

1 Heat the oil in a heavy pan, add the oats and peanuts and sauté over a medium heat for about 1 minute. Stir in the vegetables, cayenne or chillies, tomato and salt. Add the boiling water, cover and cook over a medium heat for about 5 minutes, or until the vegetables are tender.

2 Remove the pan from the heat and add the grated cheese and butter or margarine. Serve with coconut or mint chutney.

Golden Oat Bake
Yoga has been defined as 'balance of mind'. This is a very harmonizing dish. Courgettes, like oats, have a calming effect on the nervous system. Served with Spiced Spring Carrots (page 84), this is a delicious, comforting dish for a cold winter's day. Serves 6

3 tablespoons oil
50g (2oz) celery, chopped
200g (7oz) rolled oats
300g (10oz) courgettes, grated
50g (2oz) grated vegetarian cheese or
  3-4 tablespoons nutritional yeast flakes and
  15g (½oz) margarine

2 tablespoons soya flour dissolved in
  2 tablespoons water
25g (1oz) wheatgerm
50g (2oz) toasted sunflower seeds
¼ teaspoon freshly grated nutmeg
1 teaspoon salt

1 Preheat the oven to 190°C/375°F/Gas mark 5. Heat the oil in a pan and sauté the celery over a medium heat until soft. Stir in all the other ingredients and mix well.

2 Press the mixture into a well greased 900g (2lb) loaf tin. Bake in the oven for 30 minutes. Turn out to serve.

• Replace the courgette with 2 large carrots, grated. Substitute ½ teaspoon mixed herbs and ½ teaspoon celery seeds for the sunflower seeds and nutmeg.

Millet For those with gluten allergies, millet is one of the few grains that is gluten-free. It is easy to digest, with a cooling and soothing effect on the digestive system. Millet is high in vitamins and minerals, especially iron, magnesium and potassium; fibre and silicon; and helps the body in repair, cleansing and elimination. Millet can be cooked in two ways. Cooking it with plenty of water results in a thick consistency, ideal for stuffings, burgers and toppings on vegetables. If roasted first and cooked with a little less water, the result is a fluffy grain similar to couscous.

Stove-top Millet Cakes
These cakes are rather like thick pancakes. They make a full meal when served with Tomato Sauce (page 123) or Salsa (page 124), steamed vegetables and a mixed salad. Other vegetables may be substituted for the courgettes. The cakes can be reheated in a toaster. Serves 4-6

400g (14oz) millet
900ml (1½ pints) water
pinch of salt
175g (6oz) courgettes, chopped

1 teaspoon grated lemon rind
3 tablespoons wholewheat flour
2 tablespoons oil
200g (7oz) firm tofu, crumbled

1 Place the millet in a large pan with the water and salt. Bring to the boil, cover and simmer for about 30 minutes. Add the courgettes, bring back to the boil and simmer for a further 10 minutes. Leave to cool. When cold, mash the millet and courgettes. Add the remaining ingredients and stir to make a thick mixture. Add a little extra water, if necessary.

2 Heat a lightly oiled large frying pan. Cook two or three cakes at a time; for each one, place a handful of millet mixture into the pan and press it down with a wet spatula. Cook over a medium heat for 3-4 minutes on each side, until golden brown. Keep warm until they are all cooked.

Millet with Leafy Greens
Kale has 14 times more iron than red meat (gram for gram) and spinach has 11 times the amount, so this is an excellent dish for anyone worried about getting enough iron on a vegetarian diet. Serve with a salad and Spiced Spring Carrots (page 84) for a nutritious meal. Serves 6

50g (2oz) butter or margarine
300g (10oz) millet
750ml (1¼ pints) boiling water
100g (4oz) celery, finely chopped
250g (9oz) spinach and/or young kale, finely
　shredded

1 tablespoon wholewheat flour
250ml (8fl oz) warm milk or soya milk
2 tablespoons grated vegetarian cheese or
　nutritional yeast flakes
salt
pinch of freshly grated nutmeg

1 Melt half the butter or margarine in a pan and sauté the millet over a medium heat for about 5 minutes, stirring. Add the boiling water and cook gently for about 20 minutes, or until the millet is tender and all the water is absorbed. Set aside.

2 Melt the remaining butter or margarine in a separate pan and sauté the celery for 5-10 minutes, until soft. Stir in the spinach and/or kale and cook for a few minutes until wilted. Stir in the flour and add the warm milk, stirring to prevent lumps forming. Reduce the heat and cook for a few minutes. Stir in the millet and cheese or yeast flakes and season with salt and nutmeg. Mix well and serve.

Buckwheat A staple of the Eastern European diet, buckwheat is a power-packed grain containing all eight essential amino acids. It is also rich in the B vitamins, vitamin E and the bioflavonoid rutin which aids circulatory problems. A rich source of fibre and silica, buckwheat has a warming and drying effect on the body. It is astringent with very alkaline properties.

Buckwheat is fast cooking, so it is a boon to anyone with a hectic lifestyle. It can be bought either roasted (known as kasha) or unroasted. Roasted buckwheat has a richer flavour. It can be used like rice, served in stews, and with vegetables. Cooked until soft, it can be moulded into shapes and baked. Buckwheat flour is frequently used in Oriental cooking to make pancakes and noodles.

Buckwheat Burgers

Every summer we have a kids camp at our ashram in Canada. The children meditate, do asanas and practise Karma Yoga, as well as going swimming and hiking. They work up a healthy appetite and these burgers are perfectly suited for kid-sized appetites – for kids of all ages. Serve them with any sauce (pages 122-125) or on a bun. Serves 6

200g (7oz) unroasted buckwheat
450ml (15fl oz) hot water
1-2 carrots, finely diced
15g (½oz) dulse seaweed, soaked in enough
   water to cover for 5 minutes, then chopped

175g (6oz) rolled oats
3 tablespoons tamari
a little wheat, rye or rice flour
oil for brushing
sesame seeds (optional)

1 Roast the buckwheat gently for a few minutes in a dry heavy pan. When the grain starts to turn brown, add the hot water. Cover and cook for about 15 minutes. Meanwhile, preheat the oven to 200°C/400°F/Gas mark 6.

2 Remove the pan from the heat and stir in the carrots, dulse, oats and tamari. Mix well. Form the mixture into burgers. Spread the flour out on a flat plate and coat each burger, shaking to remove any excess flour. Place the burgers on a lightly greased baking sheet. Brush the tops with a little oil and sprinkle with sesame seeds, if using. Bake in the oven for about 20 minutes, until browned. Serve at once.

Kasha Varnishkas

An Eastern European speciality, this recipe was one of Swami Saradananda's childhood favourites. Serves 4-6

100g (4oz) farfalle (butterfly-shaped) pasta
100g (4oz) roasted buckwheat
750ml (1¼ pints) boiling water
1 teaspoon salt

50g (2oz) butter or margarine
Rich Brown Gravy with Vegetables (page 122),
  to serve

1 Cook the pasta in a large pan of boiling water until tender. Drain and set aside. Meanwhile, roast the buckwheat in a dry heavy pan over a low heat for a few minutes, stirring constantly. When the grain starts to turn brown, slowly add the boiling water, stirring constantly. Cover and cook over a low heat for 10-15 minutes, until tender.

2 Remove the buckwheat from the heat and mix with the salt and butter or margarine. Drain the pasta and add to the buckwheat. Serve hot with the gravy.

Japanese Buckwheat Noodles
Soba noodles, as they are popularly known in Japan, are a delight for those on a gluten-free diet who are missing the joys of pasta. Serves 4-6

250g (9oz) buckwheat noodles
7.5cm (3in) piece of kombu seaweed
200g (7oz) cabbage, shredded, or watercress
100g (4oz) peas or sweetcorn

1 carrot, chopped
1 litre (1¾ pints) water
2-3 tablespoons tamari
toasted nori seaweed, to garnish (optional)

1 Cook the noodles in a large pan of boiling water. Drain, rinse and set aside.

2 Wipe the kombu with a damp cloth to remove the excess salt, then place it in a pan with the vegetables and water and bring to the boil. Reduce the heat, cover and simmer for 5 minutes.

3 Discard the kombu and add the cooked noodles and tamari to the vegetables. Heat gently for about 2 minutes to warm the cooked noodles through again. Serve at once, garnished with a little toasted nori, if desired.

• Use wholewheat spaghetti instead of the buckwheat noodles.

Buckwheat Salad with Arame
Arame is a very mild-tasting seaweed, rich in potassium and calcium. Combined with buckwheat, it makes a lovely salad. You can make a cool version of this piquant salad using cucumber, or a crunchy version using sunflower seeds. Serves 4-6

100g (4oz) roasted buckwheat
450ml (15fl oz) water
2 tablespoons oil
1 tablespoon lemon juice
1-2 tablespoons tamari
2cm (¾in) piece of fresh root ginger, peeled and grated

¼ teaspoon pepper
1-2 tablespoons arame, soaked in enough water to cover for 10 minutes
150g (5oz) carrots, cut into matchsticks
¼ of a cucumber, cut into matchsticks or 1-2 tablespoons toasted sunflower seeds
1 tablespoon chopped fresh parsley

1 Place the buckwheat and water in a heavy pan and bring to the boil. Reduce the heat, cover the pan and simmer very gently for 15 minutes, until all the water is absorbed and the buckwheat is tender. Leave to cool.

2 Combine the oil, lemon juice, tamari, ginger and pepper to make a dressing.

3 Cut the arame into 5cm (2in) pieces and mix it into the cooled buckwheat with the carrots and cucumber or sunflower seeds and the lemon and ginger dressing. Garnish with the chopped parsley and serve at once.

Maize or Corn Alternatively considered to be a grain and a vegetable, maize has a tonic effect on the body. It is gluten-free, helps build bones and muscles, is excellent for the nervous system and brain, and may help to lower the risk of heart disease. Maize is available as corn cobs, sweetcorn kernels, cornmeal (often sold as maizemeal) and cornflour. Cornmeal can be made into porridge or used in baking. As cornmeal has a high percentage of oil, it does not keep well, so it is best to buy small quantities and use it up quickly. In parts of India, cornmeal is a staple ingredient in the rotis, or flat breads, that are prepared fresh at every meal. It is also used to thicken curries and is added to batters and vegetable dishes. Yellow cornmeal, also called polenta, is finely milled maize. It is made into a porridge which can be eaten hot or left to cool, then sliced and grilled. Cornflour is pulverized starch extracted from the grain; it is used mainly as a thickening agent.

Herbed Polenta with Fresh Corn *Polenta is a speciality of northern Italy. In this recipe, fresh corn enhances the taste of the polenta, while the rosemary adds a vibrancy to the dish. Rosemary was considered a sacred plant in ancient Greece and Rome. It is claimed to have a profound effect on the cleansing and energizing of the liver, and to improve the memory and lift depression.*
Serves 4-6

1 cob of corn	2 teaspoons finely chopped fresh rosemary
175g (6oz) yellow cornmeal	2 tablespoons olive oil
750ml (1¼ pints) water	Tomato Sauce (page 123) or Ratatouille
1 teaspoon salt	(page 89), to serve

1 Cook the corn on the cob in boiling water for 8-10 minutes, until tender. Using a sharp knife, remove the kernels and set aside.

2 Stir the cornmeal into 250ml (8fl oz) of the water to make a batter. In a large heavy pan, bring the remaining water and salt to the boil. Add the cornmeal batter all at once and stir continuously until the mixture is well blended. Add the chopped rosemary.

3 Reduce the heat so that the mixture is simmering and stir constantly for 10-15 minutes, until the polenta pulls away from the side of the pan. Add the cooked corn kernels.

4 Pour the polenta into a 25cm (10in) pie plate, smooth the top with a spatula and leave it to cool. Once set, cut the polenta into slices and fry in a little olive oil, until slightly crisp. Alternatively, brush with oil and bake or grill. Serve with tomato sauce or ratatouille.

• Serve the polenta in slices without frying or baking it.
• For extra richness and flavour, stir in 1 tablespoon olive oil while the polenta is cooking.
• Stir 2 tablespoons grated cheese into the polenta at the end of cooking.
• For a more complex flavour, omit the salt and blend in a little light miso when the polenta is cooked.

Cornbread

Cornmeal gives bread a golden colour as well as an appetizing nutty flavour and crisp texture. Use finely ground wholewheat flour (called wholewheat pastry flour), which is available from health food stores. You can vary the proportion of cornmeal and wheat flour for different tastes and consistencies. Serves 8-10

400g (14oz) cornmeal
200g (7oz) wholewheat pastry flour
1 tablespoon baking powder
1 teaspoon salt
150ml (5fl oz) oil

150ml (5fl oz) maple syrup, barley malt syrup or honey
about 350ml (12fl oz) milk or soya milk
2 tablespoons natural yoghurt (optional)

1 Preheat the oven to 190°C/375°F/Gas mark 5. Combine all the dry ingredients in a bowl. In a separate bowl, mix the wet ingredients together.

2 Mix the wet ingredients into the dry ones to make a thick pourable mixture, mixing well. If it is too thick, add more milk. Transfer to a greased 20cm (8in) square cake tin and bake in the oven for 35-40 minutes.

- Replace 150g (5oz) of the cornmeal with 150g (5oz) bran flakes.
- Make 24 small or 12 large corn muffins: spoon the mixture into muffin tins and bake at 190°C/375°F/Gas mark 5 for 15-20 minutes for small muffins, 20-25 minutes for large.

Corn Fritters

Too much fried food is not good, but occasionally the tongue may be gratified with a few of these tasty titbits. Corn fritters are a traditional Bahamian dish and they can be served with any chutney. Special thanks to Jyoti for this recipe. Makes 24-30 small fritters

175g (6oz) wholewheat flour
75g (3oz) chick pea (besan) flour
450g (1lb) fresh corn kernels (cut off the cobs) or canned sweetcorn, drained
4-6 fresh green chillies
½ teaspoon turmeric
1 teaspoon salt
¼ teaspoon pepper

juice of 1 lemon
2.5cm (1in) piece of fresh root ginger, peeled and grated
1 bunch of fresh coriander or parsley, finely chopped
3 tablespoons oil, plus oil for deep-frying
2 tablespoons natural yoghurt
½ teaspoon bicarbonate of soda

1 Mix all the ingredients, except the oil, yoghurt and bicarbonate of soda, in a heatproof bowl.

2 Heat the 3 tablespoons of oil and when it is very hot pour it over the mixture in the bowl and fold in.

3 In a separate bowl, combine the yoghurt and bicarbonate of soda, then add it to the corn to bind the mixture.

4 Heat the oil for frying. Form the mixture into little balls (about ½ tablespoon at a time) and deep-fry a few at a time in the hot oil for about 1-2 minutes, turning them with a slotted spoon. Transfer to paper towels to drain.

- Any vegetable may be substituted for, or added to, the corn. Chop the vegetable(s) into small pieces. Apples, pears or bananas with grated coconut can also be substituted.
- Add cheese or tofu to the fritter mixture, either by themselves or with fruit or vegetables.

PROTEIN
PRANA

" The foods which contain protein should not be more than one-fourth the weight of the amount of vegetables and fruit taken at a meal. Do not eat too much protein. An excess of protein over-taxes the liver and the kidneys and causes serious diseases."

Swami Sivananda

'Prana', often translated as 'life force' or 'vital energy' may be more accurately described as the energy that produces this physical manifestation. Our bodies are completely regulated by the force of prana. Each cell is controlled and built as much by prana as by protein.

To quote the Swami Vishnu-devananda in *The Complete Illustrated Book of Yoga*: "Prana is in the air, but is not the oxygen, nor any of its chemical constituents. It is in the food, water, and in the sunlight, yet it is not vitamin, heat or light-rays. Food, water and air are only the media through which the prana is carried. We absorb this prana through the food we eat, the water we drink and the air we breathe."

Food that is fresh and pure by nature is full of prana. When it is prepared with loving attention, that prana is enhanced. But if the cook is upset while cooking, the prana will be drained from the food and it won't satisfy your needs – spiritual, mental or physical.

Protein supplies the physical materials for growth and the repair of cells and tissues; as the body requires continual overhauling and renewal, a constant supply of protein is needed. Proteins are formed by the linkage of 22 different 'building blocks' called amino acids. The value of protein depends on its amino-acid content. The difference between proteins is due to the number, arrangement and proportion of the different amino acids.

Pulses (beans) are the most common sources of vegetarian protein, but nuts, seeds and cheese are also excellent. Pulses combined with grains form the basics of a vegetarian diet. Pulses are low in fat, high in fibre and rich in iron, B vitamins and trace minerals. Whereas many plants rob the soil of vital nutrients as they grow, pulses take nitrogen from the atmosphere and restore it in large amounts to the soil. By nourishing your body with pulses, you also help to nourish the planet.

In yoga, everything is best done gradually and in moderation. If you are adding pulses to your diet, start slowly, as it might take your system a while to get used to their gas-producing propensity. Aduki beans, lentils, mung beans and split peas are the easiest to digest and may be eaten on a daily basis. They may be sprouted and eaten raw. Other pulses need cooking even when sprouted, and should be eaten no more than once or twice a week.

Most pulses need soaking before cooking; wash thoroughly and pick out husks, stones or dirt, then soak in enough water to cover. After the appropriate time, drain, place the pulses in a large pan and add fresh water (the amount varies from twice the volume of pulses to four times the volume, see chart). Don't add salt, as this toughens pulses; use a little seaweed (such as kombu), if you like. Bring to the boil: if cooking aduki, black, black-eyed or kidney beans, boil vigorously for 10 minutes; if soya beans boil for 1 hour. Skim off any foam, then half cover the pan and simmer the pulses for the appropriate cooking time (see below), until soft but not mushy. About 200g (7oz) dried pulses will feed four to six people.

COOKING PULSES

Pulse	Soaking time	Volume of water	Cooking time
Aduki bean	3-4 hours	2-3 times	45-60 minutes
Black bean	3-4 hours	2-3 times	1 hour
Black-eyed bean	1-2 hours	3 times	45 minutes
Broad (fava) bean	8-12 hours	4 times	1 hour
Butter bean	8-12 hours	2-3 times	1-1½ hours
Canellini bean	4-8 hours	3 times	1-1½ hours
Chick pea	8-12 hours	4 times	1-1½ hours
Flageolet bean	8-12 hours	3 times	1-1¼ hours
Haricot	8-12 hours	3 times	1-1½ hours
Kidney bean	8-10 hours	2-3 times	1-1½ hours
Lentils (green or brown)	Not required	3 times	30-40 minutes
Mung bean	Not required	3-4 times	30-45 minutes
Pinto beans	8-12 hours	3-4 times	1-1½ hours
Puy lentils	Not required	Twice	25-35 minutes
Red lentils	Not required	Twice	15-30 minutes
Soya bean	8-12 hours	4 times	2-4 hours
Split peas	Not required	3 times	35-45 minutes

Kitcheree
People love kitcheree! This hearty one-pot dish is widely eaten in India, especially by sadhus, who leave it to cook while they are meditating. During the Sivananda Sadhana intensive course for our yoga teachers, we serve it daily. If you are doing a lot of pranayama or live in a cold climate, be sure to add the ghee. Kitcheree gives strength and vitality, and it is often used as part of a body detox programme, after kriyas (yogic cleansing exercises) and upon breaking of a fast. In Ayurveda, kitcheree often plays a key role in nutritional healing. Serves 4-6

250g (9oz) mung beans
250g (9oz) basmati rice
1 tablespoon oil
1 teaspoon brown mustard seeds
1 teaspoon cumin seeds

2 sticks of celery, finely chopped
1 teaspoon ground coriander
salt
2 tablespoons ghee (optional)

1 Place the mung beans in a pan with three to four times their volume of water. Bring to the boil, lower the heat, cover and simmer for 30-45 minutes, until tender. Meanwhile, cook the rice separately. Set these aside.

2 Heat the oil in a wok or pan. Add the mustard and cumin seeds and cook over a high heat until they 'pop'.

3 Add the celery and sauté over a medium heat for about 5 minutes. Stir in the ground coriander, cooked rice and mung beans. Cook for another 10 minutes, stirring. Season to taste with salt. Add the ghee, if using, and serve at once.

• Brown rice or barley may be substituted for the basmati rice. They both make the dish even heartier. Another popular variation at our ashram in Canada is to use pre-soaked hijiki (seaweed) instead of the celery.

Swami Gayatri's Mung Beans
The popular standby of our 70-year-young grandmother, who has taught so many people to cook and to serve with love. Serves 4

200g (7oz) mung beans
700ml (24fl oz) water
75g (3oz) desiccated coconut
2 tablespoons oil
1 teaspoon black mustard seeds

5-6 curry leaves
¼ teaspoon turmeric
1 teaspoon salt
1 heaped teaspoon ground cumin
1 teaspoon ground fennel (optional)

1 Place the mung beans in a pan with the water. Bring to the boil, lower the heat, cover and simmer for 30-45 minutes, until the beans are soft. Meanwhile, soak the coconut in a bowl with enough warm water to cover – about 50ml (2fl oz).

2 Heat the oil in a heavy frying pan. Add the mustard seeds and cook over a high heat until they 'pop'. Squeeze any water from the soaked coconut and add the coconut to the pan. Sauté gently for 2-3 minutes. Add the curry leaves, turmeric and salt and stir well for about 1 minute.

3 Drain off any excess water from the mung beans and add them to the mixture. Stir over a low heat for 2 minutes, then mix in the ground cumin and fennel. Transfer to a serving dish to serve.

White Beans with Courgette and Herbs

White beans delicately flavoured with curry powder and fennel are complemented by crisp ribbons of courgette. Serves 4-6

450g (1lb) butter beans, soaked
1 litre (1¾ pints) water
25g (1oz) butter or margarine
1 tablespoon curry powder
1 large fennel head, chopped
2 tablespoons olive oil

juice of ½ a lemon
salt and pepper
1 courgette
3 tablespoons chopped fresh parsley
3 tablespoons chopped fresh dill

1 Drain the beans, place in a pan and cover with the water. Bring to the boil. Reduce the heat, cover and simmer for 1-1½ hours, until tender.

2 Heat half of the butter or margarine in a large pan, stir in the curry powder and then sauté the fennel over a medium heat until it is translucent. Drain the beans and add them. Cover and cook over a very low heat for 10 minutes. Season the beans with the olive oil, lemon juice and salt and pepper to taste, and place in a serving dish.

3 Cut the courgette lengthwise into long ribbons. Heat the remaining butter or margarine in a frying pan, add the courgette ribbons, chopped parsley and dill and sauté gently over a medium heat, stirring frequently, until some of the courgette ribbons are lightly touched with brown. They should have softened slightly but still keep some of their 'bite' – take care not to break them. Use to garnish the beans and serve immediately.

Kamala's Pilaff *Kamala runs an affiliated Sivananda Yoga Centre in the Blue Mountains of Australia; this is one of the favourite recipes for after-satsang (group meditation) supper.* Serves 4-6

100g (4oz) yellow split peas
100g (4oz) millet
2 tablespoons ghee or oil
2 x 5cm (2in) cinnamon sticks, broken in half
½ teaspoon turmeric
½ teaspoon garam masala
1 teaspoon salt
½ teaspoon cayenne pepper (optional)

1 teaspoon ground cumin
2 tomatoes, chopped
1 litre (1¾ pints) boiling water
2 tablespoons oil
½ teaspoon black mustard seeds
250g (9oz) chopped fresh spinach,
   stalks removed

1 Wash and soak the split peas for about 2 hours. Drain well and set aside. Dry roast the millet for 5 minutes, remove from the heat and set aside. Heat the ghee or oil in a heavy frying pan. Add the cinnamon sticks, turmeric and garam masala; sauté for 8-10 minutes over a low heat. Stir in the split peas, roasted millet, salt and cayenne pepper, if using. Sauté the mixture for a further 8-10 minutes.

2 Add the ground cumin and chopped tomatoes, stir well and cook for 3-4 minutes. Add the boiling water and simmer for 30-35 minutes, stirring occasionally. About 10 minutes before the lentils are cooked, heat the oil in a separate frying pan. Add the mustard seeds and toast until they 'pop'. Add the chopped spinach; mix thoroughly, cover and simmer for 5 minutes. Add the spinach and spice mixture to the cooked split pea mixture; cover and cook over a low heat for a further 5 minutes, stirring occasionally.

Swami Saradananda's Baked Beans
This is a traditional New England-style slow-cooking dish – put it in the oven in the morning and forget about it until almost dinner time, apart from checking it from time to time. Navy or pinto beans may be substituted to equally satisfy nutritional needs and hungry appetites. Serve with Cornbread (page 65) or rice. Serves 6

200g (7oz) kidney beans, soaked
800ml (28fl oz) hot water
2 bay leaves, crumbled
150ml (5fl oz) molasses
1 teaspoon mustard powder

10 black peppercorns, crushed slightly
4 tablespoons tomato purée
1 potato, chopped
1 carrot, grated
1 teaspoon salt

1 Preheat the oven to 140°C/275°F/Gas mark 1. Drain the beans and place in a pan with the hot water. Bring to the boil and boil vigorously for 10 minutes. Skim off the white foam. Transfer the beans and cooking water to a casserole dish.

2 Add the bay leaves, molasses, mustard powder and peppercorns. Cover the dish with a tight fitting lid and cook in the oven for 6-8 hours, checking from time to time to make sure that there is enough water.

3 Add the tomato purée, potato, carrot and salt. Increase the oven temperature to 150°C/300°F/Gas mark 2 and cook for another 2 hours. Serve hot.

• After cooking, turn off the oven and leave the covered casserole dish inside overnight for 'Beans on Toast' in the morning.

Prema and Dattatreya's Cinnamon Beans
Dattatreya, a 73-year-young yogi who can still put both legs behind his head, is a native of Italy. Now teaching yoga in London, he and his wife Prema have adapted this Italian dish. It is always a favourite at our Christmas party. It is especially nice served with Herbed Polenta with Fresh Corn (page 64). Serves 4

225g (8oz) black-eyed beans, soaked
400g (14oz) tomatoes
4 tablespoons olive oil
2.5cm (1in) piece of fresh root ginger, peeled and grated

4 sticks of celery, finely chopped
250ml (8fl oz) water
2 teaspoons tomato purée
2 teaspoons ground cinnamon
salt and pepper to taste

1 Drain the beans, place in a pan and cover with fresh water. Bring to the boil and boil vigorously for 10 minutes. Half cover and simmer for 45 minutes, until tender.

2 Scald and skin the tomatoes and chop them.

3 Heat the oil in a pan over a low heat. Add the ginger and celery and fry gently for 2-3 minutes. Drain the beans and add to the pan with the water, tomato purée, cinnamon and salt and pepper. Stir gently and cook for a further 15 minutes. Add the tomatoes and cook for a further 5 minutes. Serve at once.

Chilli con Veggies
A tasty dish that can assist in making the changes in diet (and lifestyle) gradually, as is usually best in the long term. Even non-vegetarian friends will love it served with Cornbread (page 65). Vary the dish sometimes by using black beans instead of kidney beans. Serves 4-6

200g (7oz) kidney beans, soaked
4 tablespoons oil
1½ teaspoons chilli powder
½ teaspoon ground cumin
½ teaspoon turmeric
1 large green pepper, cored, seeded and chopped

3 sticks of celery, chopped
1 large carrot, chopped
2 large tomatoes, chopped
4 tablespoons tomato purée
2-3 tablespoons lemon juice (optional)
salt to taste

1 Drain the kidney beans, place in a pan and cover with fresh water. Bring to the boil and boil vigorously for 10 minutes. Half cover and simmer gently for a further 1-1½ hours, until the beans are tender. Drain and set aside.

2 Heat the oil in a heavy frying pan and sauté the spices for a few minutes. Add the green pepper, celery and carrots and cook for 4-5 minutes, until the vegetables are slightly soft. Stir in the tomatoes and tomato purée; simmer for 15 minutes. Add the cooked beans and simmer for 15 minutes. Season with lemon juice and salt and serve at once.

Spanish-style Chick Peas
Chick peas are best eaten as a midday meal. When served as the evening meal they tend to make getting up for morning meditation more difficult. Serves 4-6

225g (8oz) chick peas, soaked
3 tablespoons olive oil
pinch of ground coriander
pinch of ground ginger
pinch of freshly grated nutmeg
1 green pepper, cored, seeded and chopped

1 red pepper, cored, seeded and chopped
1 fresh green chilli, seeded and chopped
  (optional)
450g (1lb) tomatoes, chopped
1 teaspoon salt
¼ teaspoon pepper

1 Drain the chick peas, place in a pan and cover with fresh water. Add 1 tablespoon of the olive oil. Bring to the boil, half cover and simmer for about 1-1½ hours, until the chick peas are tender. Drain and set aside.

2 Heat the remaining oil in a heavy frying pan. Add the spices, peppers, green chilli, if using, and tomatoes and sauté until the vegetables are tender. Add the chick peas to them and mix well, then cook together for about 2 minutes. Season with the salt and pepper and serve at once.

Aduki Bean Stew

Aduki beans are used extensively in Japanese cooking. This is a classic macrobiotic dish, best served on rice or millet. Serves 4-6

175g (6oz) aduki beans, soaked
2 bay leaves (optional)
900ml (1½ pints) water
300g (10oz) acorn or butternut squash, peeled, seeded and cut into small cubes

1 carrot, cubed or sliced
½ teaspoon dried thyme
1 teaspoon dried savory (optional)
2-4 tablespoons miso

1 Drain the beans and place in a pan with the bay leaves and water. Cook over a medium heat for about 40 minutes, until almost tender, adding a little more water if necessary.

2 Add the squash, carrot, thyme and savory, if using. Continue to simmer for about 20 minutes, until everything is tender, stirring occasionally. The stew should have a slightly dry consistency. Remove the pan from the heat and stir in the miso. Serve at once.

• Omit the bay leaves; add 15g (½oz) pre-soaked hijiki at the same time as the vegetables.

Tamale-Bean Pie

This tasty Mexican pie is soft so it needs to be spooned rather than sliced. Serve with a green salad. Serves 4-6

200g (7oz) pinto beans, soaked
750ml (1¼ pints) water
2 tablespoons oil
1 teaspoon black mustard seeds
2 teaspoons cumin seeds
1 large green pepper, cored, seeded and chopped
2-3 fresh green chillies, seeded and chopped
4 tomatoes, chopped

1 teaspoon cayenne pepper
1 teaspoon dried oregano
½-1 teaspoon salt
Crust:
250g (9oz) cornmeal
250ml (8fl oz) cold water
1 teaspoon salt
750ml (1¼ pints) boiling water

1 Drain the beans, place in a pan and cover with the water. Cook over a medium heat, half covered, for 1-1½ hours, until tender. Set aside.

2 Heat the oil in a large frying pan. Add the mustard and cumin seeds and roast over a high heat until they 'pop'. Add the green pepper and chillies and sauté until slightly soft. Stir in the tomatoes, cayenne pepper and oregano and cook until the tomatoes are soft. Add the salt and pinto beans. Cook over a low heat for about 10 minutes, stirring occasionally. Set aside.

3 To make the crust, combine the cornmeal, cold water and salt in a non-stick pan, mixing well. Place over a medium heat, add the boiling water and stir until smooth. Continue cooking for about 15 minutes, stirring occasionally. Meanwhile, preheat the oven to 180°C/350°F/Gas mark 4.

4 Oil a casserole dish or large round pie plate and spread half of the cornmeal mixture on the bottom and around the sides to form a shell. Spoon the bean mixture into the shell and top with the remaining cornmeal. Cover the dish or pie plate with a lid or foil and bake in the oven for about 30 minutes. Serve hot.

Lentil Dal
Often mistaken for a soup, dal is served over rice and/or with chapatis as the standard meal of northern India. For a simple meal, serve it with plain rice, yoghurt and Curried Vegetables (page 88). For a larger spread, add Rice Pilau (page 47), raita and Chapatis (page 53). For a more aromatic dal, add a cinnamon stick and/or 5 or 6 cloves to the lentils while cooking. Serves 4-6

200g (7oz) red lentils
750ml (1¼ pints) water
1 teaspoon turmeric
1 bay leaf
1-2 tablespoons ghee, butter or oil
1 teaspoon mustard seeds

1 teaspoon cumin or fennel seeds
2 teaspoons ground coriander
2 tomatoes, coarsely chopped
1 teaspoon salt
½-1 tablespoon lemon juice (optional)
4 tablespoons chopped fresh coriander

1 Place the lentils in a pan with the water, turmeric and bay leaf. Simmer for 15-20 minutes, until the lentils are tender.

2 Meanwhile, heat the ghee, butter or oil in a heavy frying pan. Add the mustard and cumin or fennel seeds and cook over a high heat until they 'pop'.

3 Add the ground coriander and tomatoes and cook for another 5 minutes, then add the mixture to the cooked lentils. Add more water if the mixture is too thick, or cook a little longer to make it thicker. Add the salt and lemon juice, if desired. Stir in the chopped coriander and serve at once.

Carrot Cashew Slice
Carrots are renowned for strengthening the eyesight, celery for its calming effect on the nerves, and cabbage for its all-round healing properties. Serve with a simple boiled grain and a green salad. Topped with Tomato Sauce (page 123), it becomes a festive meal. Serves 4-6

250g (9oz) millet
600ml (1 pint) water
250g (9oz) cashew nut pieces
2 tablespoons oil
4 carrots, grated
½ white cabbage, finely chopped

4 sticks of celery, finely sliced
1 tablespoon mixed herbs
½ teaspoon freshly grated nutmeg
1 tablespoon tamari
pinch of pepper

1 Place the millet in a large pan with the water. Simmer for 30-40 minutes, until tender.

2 Heat a dry frying pan and roast the cashews over a high heat for about 5 minutes, until lightly browned. Set aside.

3 Meanwhile, preheat the oven to 220°C/425°F/Gas mark 7.

4 Heat the oil in a pan, add the vegetables and sauté over a medium heat for about 15 minutes, until the vegetables are soft.

5 Add the cooked millet, roasted cashews, mixed herbs, nutmeg, tamari and pepper and mix well. Spoon into an oiled 450g (1lb) loaf tin and bake in the oven for 15 minutes.

6 Leave to cool, then turn out of the tin. Cut into slices and serve.

Vegetable Pâté
Developed by Uma at the Sivananda Yoga Retreat in Nassau, this recipe is a favourite which has been passed from centre to centre. It is best cooked in advance and allowed to chill for a few hours. Serves 6-8

100g (4oz) sunflower seeds
75g (3oz) wholewheat flour
15g (½oz) nutritional yeast flakes
2 tablespoons lemon juice
25g (1oz) butter or margarine
2 carrots
1 potato
1 stick of celery

pinch of dried sage
1½ teaspoons dried thyme
1½ teaspoons dried basil or a bunch of fresh basil
1 teaspoon salt
250ml (8fl oz) warm water
dash of pepper

1 Preheat the oven to 200°C/400°F/Gas mark 6. Put all the ingredients into a food processor and blend for about 4 minutes, until smooth. Alternatively, grate all the vegetables, grind the seeds in a blender and mix everything together in a bowl.

2 Spoon the vegetable mixture into an oiled 450g (1lb) loaf tin and bake in the oven for 1 hour. Leave to cool, then chill it in the refrigerator before serving. The pâté rises while cooking, but sinks as it cools.

• Substitute almonds, walnuts, or a mixture, for the sunflower seeds.

Sunflower Sesame Rissoles
After Christmas at our Centre in London we have a Beginners' Week. After a few days of ashram life, the experienced 'Karma Yogis' prepare the New Year's Eve feast. This party recipe was made by Gloria MacDonald. It is very nice served with Tomato Sauce (page 123) or Rich Brown Gravy (page 122). Serves 4-6

225g (8oz) sesame seeds
225g (8oz) sunflower seeds
½ teaspoon dried marjoram
½ teaspoon dried oregano
½ teaspoon dried thyme
½ teaspoon dried basil
1 teaspoon ground cumin

1 tablespoon tamari
1 large green pepper, cored, seeded and finely chopped
1-2 sticks of celery, finely chopped
1 carrot, grated
1 tomato, quartered

1 Preheat the oven to 180°C/350°F/Gas 4. Grind the sesame seeds in a blender, then the sunflower seeds, making sure both lots are not too finely ground as the rissoles need some texture. Put the seeds in a large bowl.

2 Mix in the herbs, cumin and tamari, then the green pepper, celery and carrot. Put the tomato into the blender and blend briefly, allowing small lumps to remain. Carefully stir the tomato into the seed mixture.

3 Take a handful of the mixture, form it into a smooth ball and flatten it. Place it on a greased baking sheet. Repeat to make 12-16 rissoles. Bake the rissoles in the oven for 30-45 minutes, until browned.

• Make smaller rissoles and serve them as party food with dips.

Tempeh This is a soya food which is sold in densely packed cakes. Originating from Indonesia, tempeh has a stronger and more satisfying flavour than tofu, making it ideal for casseroles and stews. It has a high protein and vitamin B12 content, and is sold chilled or frozen. Different varieties are made by combining soya beans with wheat, rice, millet, peanuts and/or coconut. Like its cousin tofu, it is very versatile and can be baked, fried, marinated and steamed. It can be pan-fried with herbs or spices and tossed into pasta, or added to grain dishes at the last moment. Highly nutritious, tempeh can be of benefit to frail people. Do not eat it raw; it needs to be thoroughly cooked.

Tempeh Stew *Serve this stew in bowls with cooked rice or barley or large chunks of fresh bread.* Serves 6

1 carrot, cubed or thinly sliced
1 turnip, cubed or thinly sliced
¾ of a swede, cubed
½ a small cabbage, shredded
1 marrow, cubed
1 strip of kombu seaweed, cut into
  small pieces

1 tablespoon fresh root ginger, peeled and grated
400ml (14fl oz) water
1-2 tablespoons arrowroot
2 tablespoons oil
275g (9½oz) tempeh, cut into thick strips
tamari

1 Put the vegetables, kombu, ginger and 300ml (10fl oz) of the water into a heavy pan, half cover and simmer for about 10 minutes, until the vegetables are half cooked.

2 Put the remaining water in a small bowl and blend in 1 tablespoon arrowroot until it is smooth. Stir this into the stew and continue stirring until it thickens. (If it comes back to the boil and has not thickened, repeat the process.) Continue cooking until all the vegetables are tender. Meanwhile, heat the oil in a separate pan and sauté the tempeh until golden brown. Add it to the stew just before serving. Season to taste with tamari.

Tempeh with Sesame Seeds *This light dish can be served with a simple grain. Tofu can be substituted for the tempeh.* Serves 3-4

225g (8oz) tempeh, cut into strips
2 tablespoons olive oil or dark sesame oil
2-3 tablespoon sesame seeds
Sauce:
1 tablespoon oil
3-4 tomatoes, chopped

2 teaspoons grated fresh root ginger
2 tablespoons sesame seeds
250ml (8fl oz) water, plus 1-2 tablespoons
75ml (3fl oz) tamari
1 tablespoon arrowroot or cornflour

1 Preheat the oven to 180°C/350°F/Gas mark 4. Coat the tempeh with olive or sesame oil and sesame seeds. Place the tempeh on a baking sheet and bake in the oven for 45-60 minutes, until browned, turning the strips two or three times.

2 For the sauce, heat the oil in a pan and sauté the tomatoes, ginger and sesame seeds over a medium heat for 2-3 minutes. Add the 250ml (8fl oz) water and the tamari and simmer for about 10 minutes. Mix the arrowroot with the remaining 1-2 tablespoons water and add to the sauce, stirring until it thickens. Serve the sauce with the baked tempeh.

Tempeh Stew

Tofu Also known as bean curd, tofu has become one of the most popular soya foods available. Its versatility and nutritional richness have made it an essential ingredient in vegetarian kitchens. It is extremely high in protein, iron, calcium and phosphorus, and has very little cholesterol. There are several varieties available, ranging in texture from extra firm to silken. Firm tofu is the most versatile and best for stir-frying and baking. If you are going to make creamier dishes, choose silken tofu which has a wonderfully smooth texture almost akin to yoghurt. Tofu can be used in many recipes as a substitute for dairy products such as cheese and cream, and because of its neutral flavour can be used in savoury or sweet dishes. Buy the freshest available and make sure that genetically modified soya beans have not been used in its manufacture. Keep tofu covered in cold water in the refrigerator. For health reasons, it is best not to eat raw tofu unless you have made it yourself; if using it in uncooked dishes, steam the tofu for a few minutes first.

Crispy Baked Tofu
Serve this tasty bake with brown rice, millet or any of the grain dishes on pages 47-65. Serves 4-6

450g (1lb) firm tofu
25-40g (1-1½oz) butter or margarine

2-3 tablespoons tamari
nutritional yeast flakes for sprinkling

1 Preheat the oven to 190°C/375°F/Gas mark 5. Slice the tofu into eight or 12 pieces.

2 Melt the butter or margarine in a pan, remove from the heat and add the tamari.

3 Place the tofu pieces on a baking sheet and brush with the tamari and butter or margarine mixture. Sprinkle with the yeast flakes and bake in the oven for 20 minutes, or until the tofu is lightly roasted and crispy.

• **Baked Marinated Tofu:** For moister tofu with some sauce, combine 2 tablespoons toasted sesame oil or melted butter or margarine, with 2 tablespoons tamari, 2 tablespoons grated root ginger and 4 tablespoons water. Pour this mixture over the tofu pieces in a dish and leave to marinate for 1 hour. Place in the oven with the marinade. Cover the dish with a lid or foil and bake as above. Serve with anything.

Tofu Carrot Mousse
This is a wonderful way to use winter vegetables. Serve with steamed new potatoes and a crisp salad. Serves 6

2 tablespoons sesame oil
2-3 carrots, sliced
1 small swede or 1 parsnip, roughly chopped
125ml (4fl oz) water

1-2 tablespoons tamari
250g (9oz) firm tofu
toasted sesame seeds or chopped fresh parsley, to garnish (optional)

1 Preheat the oven to 200°C/400°F/Gas mark 6. Heat the sesame oil in a pan and sauté the carrots and swede or parsnip over a medium heat for 5 minutes. Add the water and tamari and simmer until the vegetables are tender.

2 Transfer the vegetables to a food processor or blender, add the tofu and blend until smooth. Spoon the mixture into a 600ml (1 pint) baking dish and bake in the oven for about 30 minutes, until just firm. Leave to cool, then garnish with sesame seeds or parsley before serving.

Sweet and Sour Tofu
This is delicious with just a bowl of rice or it can be served as part of a Chinese feast. Serves 4-6

450g (1lb) firm tofu
2 tablespoons tamari
kuzu, arrowroot or cornflour for coating (optional)
4 tablespoons sesame oil
1 green pepper, cored, seeded and chopped
1 stick celery, cut into 2.5cm (1in) diagonal slices
1 carrot, sliced diagonally
100g (4oz) mange-tout, sliced diagonally
100g (4oz) bamboo shoots, cut into wedges

150g (5oz) water chestnuts, sliced
100g (4oz) fresh pineapple, diced
Sauce:
2 tablespoons cornflour or arrowroot
125ml (4fl oz) water
3 tablespoons honey
4 tablespoons tamari
2 tablespoons lemon juice
4 tablespoons tomato purée

1 Wrap the tofu in a clean tea-towel. Place a chopping board or heavy book on top and leave for 30 minutes to press out the liquid. Cut the tofu into 2.5-5cm (1-2in) cubes and sprinkle them with tamari. Coat with kuzu, arrowroot or cornflour, if using.

2 Heat 2 tablespoons of the sesame oil in a wok or frying pan and fry the tofu until crisp; set aside (preferably keep warm in a low oven).

3 Heat the remaining oil in the wok and stir-fry the green pepper, celery, carrot and mange-tout for 5 minutes, until the vegetables are tender but still firm. Stir in the bamboo shoots, water chestnuts and pineapple and cook for 2-3 minutes. Remove the vegetables and keep warm.

4 To make the sauce, dissolve the cornflour or arrowroot in the water. Combine the remaining sauce ingredients in a separate bowl and add to the wok. When the sauce starts to boil, add the cornflour or arrowroot mixture and stir for 2 minutes, or until the sauce thickens. Add the fried tofu and vegetables, mix well and serve at once.

Tofu, Pasta and Olives
This is tofu in Mediterranean guise, made into a creamy sauce to serve with pasta. Silken tofu is best but the firm variety will do. This quantity of olives gives the sauce a wonderful flavour, but you can reduce the amount or substitute sun-dried tomatoes for some of the olives. Serves 4-6

450g (1lb) silken tofu
2 tablespoons olive oil
100g (4oz) celery, chopped
200g (7oz) kale or spinach, chopped
½ teaspoon each of dried basil, oregano, thyme

1 bay leaf
450g (1lb) dried pasta
4 tablespoons light miso
200g (7oz) black olives, stoned and sliced
200g (7oz) green olives, stoned and sliced
pepper

1 Poach the tofu for 3 minutes in a small pan of simmering water. Drain and set aside.

2 Heat the olive oil in a heavy frying pan and add the celery, kale or spinach and herbs. Stir-fry for 3-4 minutes, then reduce the heat to low and cook for a further 6-7 minutes or until the celery is soft, stirring occasionally. Discard the bay leaf. Cook the pasta in a large pan of boiling water for about 8-10 minutes, until *al dente* (tender but firm to the bite).

3 Transfer the vegetable mixture to a food processor or blender, add the tofu and miso and blend to a smooth and creamy sauce. Stir in the black and green olives. Drain the cooked pasta and immediately toss it with the tofu mixture. Season with pepper and serve.

VEGETABLE VIRYA

"Mother Nature has demonstrated her marvellous skill and power in cultivating these wonderful vegetables for her children in her cosmic garden. How kind and merciful She is; She has compounded and beautifully blended all the essentials of life in various kinds of vegetables to give proper strength, vitality, vigour and energy to Her children."

Swami Sivananda

Virya is the physical and mental energy that is necessary to prosper in any walk of life. Even for spiritual pursuits, vibrant vitality is a prerequisite. Without it, you cannot penetrate into the hidden depths of the vast ocean of life within and attain the final beatitude. Without good health, you cannot wage war with the turbulent senses and boisterous mind. Inner strength, or virya, is the drive that carries one along the path, bouncing back after failures and maintaining courage through even the most difficult times.

Along with the intake of dietary vitamins that are found so abundantly in vegetables, the yogi, attempting to maintain virya, should also partake of 'philosophical vitamins', as expressed by Swami Sivananda:

Vitamin A: adaptability, austerity

Vitamin B: bravery, balance of mind, bhakti (devotion)

Vitamin C: compassion, consideration, charity, courage, co-operation, cleanliness, contemplation, contentment, concentration

Vitamin D: diligence, discipline, detachment

Vitamin E: equanimity, edurance

Vitamin F: faith, forgiveness, friendliness, firmness, fasting, fortitude, fearlessness, forbearance, frankness

Vitamin K: kindness, knowledge

Vitamin P: patience, perseverance, purity, politeness

"Vegetables are the most important sources of vitamins in every diet – especially those that can be eaten raw. The humble tomato because of its wealth of the three main types of vitamins (A, B and C), is considered, along with lettuce, spinach and cabbage, one of the elect, one of the big four, that head the vegetable kingdom."

Swami Vishnu-devananda

Vegetables are also our main sources of valuable minerals (such as iron and potassium) that act as eliminators, antiseptics, blood purifiers and producers of electromagnetic energy. They also help to keep an alkaline reserve in the body, which is essential for maintaining the blood's capacity for carrying carbon dioxide to the lungs for elimination. They aid the digestion and assimilation of the proteins in pulses, and supply fibre. Leafy and juicy vegetables help to prevent the blood from becoming too acid by balancing the acid-generating sugars, fats, proteins and starches.

Steaming is the simplest and healthiest way of cooking vegetables to prevent loss of nutrients, preserving maximum prana, natural flavour and texture. Wash vegetables in cold water and peel ones like carrots if they are not organic. Vegetables can be cut horizontally or lengthwise; it makes an attractive dish if you vary the types of slices, cubes and batons. Put about 250ml (8fl oz) water into a wok or steamer and bring to the boil. Place the vegetables in a steamer basket over the water, cover tightly and steam for 5-10 minutes. Do not overcook; steamed vegetables should be crisp and retain their natural colour. Vegetables may be steamed individually, or several varieties together. Cook similar types together; for example, root vegetables will need longer than seeded vegetables, and both will need longer than leafy greens.

Stir-frying is another quick, healthy way of cooking vegetables. Allow a good handful of vegetables per person – favourites or seasonal ones. Wash, trim and cut into bite-sized pieces. Vegetables should stay crisp, not become limp and overcooked; cook them in the same order as for steaming.

Vegetables can also be baked; potatoes are the favourite, but other root or strong-flavoured vegetables can be baked whole or cut into pieces and baked in foil parcels.

Spiced Spring Carrots
This recipe was devised by Jyoti, our Irish teacher at the London Centre. Carrots are rich in vitamin A, purify the blood and tone the kidneys. Crushed hazelnuts can be substituted for the almonds. Serves 4

4 carrots, cut into matchsticks
50g (2oz) flaked almonds
50g (2oz) butter or margarine
1 teaspoon ground cumin

2 teaspoons chopped fresh coriander
1 teaspoon clear honey
salt and pepper (optional)

1 Steam the carrot sticks for about 10 minutes, until tender but still crunchy. Meanwhile, set aside a few of the flaked almonds and roast the remainder in a dry heavy pan over a high heat, until golden brown around the edges.

2 Melt the butter or margarine in a pan and cook the cumin over a high heat for a few seconds to release the aroma, being careful to not burn it. Take the pan off the heat and add the carrots, browned almonds and coriander. Mix well, then stir in the honey. Add a pinch of salt and pepper, if desired. Serve at once, garnished with the reserved almonds.

Exotic Aubergine and Mange-tout *This half*

*Chinese-half Indian dish marries the smoothness of aubergine with the crispness of
mange-tout. This combination of contrasting textures can be seen to symbolize the
totality of Nature.* Serves 4

1 aubergine, peeled and cut into 2cm (¾in)
   cubes
salt (optional)
3 tablespoons oil
1 teaspoon black mustard seeds
1 teaspoon chopped fresh ginger
¼ teaspoon ground coriander
¼ teaspoon ground cumin

¼ teaspoon ground turmeric
250g (9oz) mange-tout, sliced diagonally into
   2cm (¾in) pieces
125ml (4fl oz) water
1 small tomato, chopped
2 teaspoons lemon juice
2 tablespoons tamari

1 If liked, sprinkle the aubergine cubes with salt and leave to drain for 1 hour. Rinse and pat dry.
This removes some of the bitterness and cuts down on the oil absorbed.

2 Heat the oil in a heavy frying pan or wok. Add the mustard seeds and ginger and cook over a
high heat until the mustard seeds 'pop'. Add the rest of the spices and sauté over a medium
heat for about 5 minutes. Stir in the aubergine and mange-tout, turning them to coat with spices.

3 Add the water, cover and cook until the vegetables are soft and cooked, at most 8 minutes.
Remove from heat, add the chopped tomato, lemon juice and tamari. Cover the pan again and
leave to stand for a few minutes before serving.

Long Beans in Black Bean Sauce *Long beans*

*have more body than common green beans and cooking them in black bean sauce
increases the protein value of this vegetable dish. Fresh long beans and salted black
beans are available from Chinese food stores. Serve the beans with brown rice for a
simple, nourishing meal. For an impressive Chinese meal, serve with Sweet and Sour
Tofu (page 81), preceded by Tofu Vegetable Soup Orientale (page 42).* Serves 4-6

2 tablespoons oil
450g (1lb) long beans, trimmed and cut into
   5cm (2in) pieces
2-3 tablespoons mashed salted black beans
1 tablespoon tamari

1 tablespoon honey
50ml (2fl oz) water, plus 1 tablespoon
1 tablespoon cornflour or arrowroot
roasted sesame seeds for sprinkling

1 Heat the oil in a wok or heavy frying pan and stir-fry the long beans over a high heat for about
2 minutes.

2 Combine the black beans, tamari, honey and the 50ml (2fl oz) water. Add this mixture to the
long beans and cook for 2 minutes.

3 Dissolve the cornflour or arrowroot in the remaining 1 tablespoon water, stir it into the beans
and cook for 2 minutes. Sprinkle with roasted sesame seeds and serve at once.

• Use green beans instead of long beans.

Gnocchi with Spinach and Basil Sauce

These tender little Italian dumplings are much nicer when home-made and make a delightful alternative to pasta dishes. You can use fresh or canned tomatoes. Serves 6

1kg (2¼lb) potatoes, chopped
salt
1 tablespoon chopped fresh basil
175g (6oz) wholewheat flour
water or oil for mixing (optional)
grated vegetarian cheese, to serve (optional)
basil leaves, to garnish

Sauce:
1½ tablespoons olive oil
1-2 sticks of celery, finely chopped
600g (1lb 5oz) plum tomatoes, chopped
1½ tablespoons tomato purée
350g (12oz) finely chopped spinach
25g (1oz) chopped fresh basil or 3 tablespoons
  dried basil
pepper

1 Cook the potatoes in a pan of salted boiling water for 15 minutes, or until tender. Drain and press through a sieve. Stir in the tablespoon of basil and gradually add the flour. Mix to a soft dough, adding a little water or oil if the mixture is too stiff, or more flour if it is too wet.

2 Cool slightly, then knead the dough lightly until smooth. Divide it into quarters and shape each portion into a roll, 40cm (16in) long and 2.5cm (1in) in diameter. Cut the dough into 2cm (¾in) lengths and press a fork lightly into each one to make a pattern. Place them on a floured surface and leave to dry for 10-15 minutes.

3 Meanwhile, make the sauce. Heat the olive oil and sauté the celery until softened. Add the tomatoes, tomato purée and spinach; cook uncovered over a medium heat for 5-10 minutes, stirring occasionally. Add the basil and season to taste with salt and pepper. Keep warm.

4 Cook the gnocchi, in batches, in boiling water for 2-3 minutes, or until they rise to the surface. Keep warm until they are all cooked. Top with the sauce and serve at once. Sprinkle with a little cheese, if desired, and garnish with basil leaves.

Latkes
These potato pancakes, a mainstay of Jewish cuisine, are a wonderful source of energy and are rich in vitamin C and potassium. If you don't want to grate the potatoes and turnips, dice them and then purée in a food processor. Baking the latkes means they are not as crisp as fried ones, but they are less oily. Serve with apple sauce and/or soured cream or yoghurt. Serves 6

6 potatoes, finely grated
1 large turnip, finely grated
1 teaspoon mustard powder
2 teaspoons baking powder

150g (5oz) matzo meal or fresh wholewheat
  breadcrumbs, plus a little extra if necessary
¼ teaspoon salt

1 Preheat the oven to 190°C/375°F/Gas mark 5. Drain the potatoes thoroughly to remove all excess water. Place them in a bowl and add the turnip, mustard powder, baking powder, matzo meal or breadcrumbs and salt. Mix well, adding more matzo meal or crumbs if necessary to bind.

2 Using your hands, shape the mixture into small rounds, about 4cm (1¾in) in diameter. Place them on a baking sheet and bake in the oven for about 20 minutes, until crisp on the bottom, then turn over and bake for another 20 minutes, until both sides are crisp. They should be crisp on the outside and soft on the inside.

Curried Vegetables

The name 'curry' can be used to refer to any dish of vegetables cooked in a spicy sauce. In northern India, the spices are usually cooked in a tomato base. In the south, grated coconut is frequently used instead of tomato. This basic recipe can be adapted to use whatever vegetables you have to hand. It can be served as part of a simple Indian meal with plain rice, Lentil Dal (page 76) and Chapatis (page 53). Serves 4-6

2 tablespoons oil
1 teaspoon black mustard seeds
¼ teaspoon turmeric
1 teaspoon curry powder
1 tomato, chopped

1 cauliflower, separated into small florets
2 potatoes, cubed and par-boiled
50ml (2fl oz) water
lemon juice to taste (optional)
1 teaspoon salt

1 Heat the oil in a large pan and roast the mustard seeds over a high heat until they 'pop'. Add the turmeric and curry powder and stir well. Reduce the heat, add the chopped tomato and cook for 3-4 minutes, until soft.

2 Add the cauliflower, stirring gently to coat the florets with the spices. Stir in the potatoes, water, lemon juice and salt. Cover and cook for 15-20 minutes, until the potatoes and cauliflower are just tender. Add a little more water if necessary to prevent the mixture drying out. Serve hot.

• Omit the cauliflower to use as a traditional stuffing for Masala Dosa (page 28).
• Replace the cauliflower with 300-400g (10-14oz) vegetables of your choice.

Bavarian Red Cabbage

The deep red of the cabbage with the hint of cloves and cinnamon makes this elegantly simple dish a perennial favourite at the very busy Sivananda Yoga Centre in Munich. Serves 4-6

1 tablespoon oil or 15g (½oz) butter or margarine
1 small red cabbage, coarsely shredded
1 carrot, grated
150ml (5fl oz) water
6 whole cloves

2 slivers of cinnamon stick
juice of 1 lemon
½ teaspoon salt
pepper to taste (optional)

Heat the oil, butter or margarine in a heavy pan and sauté the cabbage and carrot over a medium heat for 5 minutes. Add the water and spices. Cover and cook for about 30 minutes, until the cabbage is tender. Season with the lemon juice, salt and pepper and serve warm.

• The cabbage and spices can be baked in a moderate oven instead of on the top of the cooker, if preferred.

Indian-style Cabbage
This delicately spiced dish goes well with Lentil Dal (page 76) and plain rice or Chapatis (see page 53). For a more elegant North Indian meal, serve it with Rice Pilau (page 47) and Curried Vegetables (see opposite), using courgettes instead of cauliflower. Serves 4-6

1 potato, diced
2 tablespoons oil or ghee (or half and half)
1 tablespoon mustard seeds
1½ teaspoons cumin seeds
1 teaspoon ground coriander

½ teaspoon turmeric
dash of cayenne pepper
1 cabbage, finely chopped
1 teaspoon salt

1 Steam the diced potato for 5-10 minutes to part-cook; set aside. Heat the oil in a heavy frying pan, add the mustard seeds and cook over a high heat until they 'pop'. Add the other spices, then sauté over a medium heat for 1-2 minutes.

2 Add the cabbage, stir well and cook until the cabbage is soft. Add the part-cooked potatoes and salt and cook for about 5 minutes, until the potatoes are cooked; the dish should be fairly dry. Serve at once.

Ratatouille
All the vegetables can be sautéed together if you are in a hurry, but the flavour is better if you roast the aubergine and courgettes first to bring out their very distinctive flavours. The grated carrot is added to balance the acidity of the tomatoes. Serve the ratatouille over pasta or rice and sprinkle with grated cheese, if desired. For a complete meal, serve with a green salad as well. Serves 4-6

1 aubergine, cut into large chunks
2-3 courgettes, cut into large chunks
extra virgin olive oil
salt and pepper
2 sticks of celery, finely chopped
1 red pepper, cored, seeded and cut into strips

1 carrot, grated
3 large juicy tomatoes, chopped
1 tablespoon tomato purée
2 tablespoons chopped fresh basil or
  1 tablespoon dried oregano or basil

1 Preheat the oven to 200°C/400°F/Gas mark 6. Place the aubergine and courgettes in a baking dish greased with olive oil. Brush with more olive oil, sprinkle with salt and pepper and bake in the oven for 20-30 minutes, until the vegetables are tender.

2 Meanwhile, heat 1 tablespoon of olive oil in a pan and sauté the celery over a medium heat for 2-3 minutes, then add the red pepper and cook until softened. Add the grated carrot, tomatoes, tomato purée and herbs and cook for 5 minutes.

3 Add the tomato mixture to the baked vegetables. Taste and adjust the seasoning, if necessary, before serving.

Baked Butternut Squash

This is a cool weather favourite at the Sivananda Yoga Ranch in upstate New York. Butternut squash has a glorious colour reminiscent of the glowing autumn foliage and its creamy sweet flavour enlivens any meal on a cold evening. Rich in vitamin A, squash is also known to soothe acidic stomachs and help counteract the effects of ill-considered foods. Serves 4-6

1 butternut squash or 2 acorn squash
50g (2oz) butter or margarine, melted
100g (4oz) wholewheat breadcrumbs
¼ teaspoon freshly grated nutmeg

½ teaspoon ground cinnamon
2 large eating apples, peeled and cut into chunks

1 Preheat the oven to 180°C/350°F/Gas mark 4. Cut the squash in half; remove the seeds and stringy bits.

2 Mix the melted butter or margarine with the breadcrumbs, spices and apples and spoon this mixture into the squash halves. Place them in a roasting tin, cover with foil and bake for about 45 minutes. Remove the foil and bake for a further 10 minutes to brown the top. Serve hot.

Creamy Baked Fennel

Fennel is a diuretic and helps to clear the lungs. Here, its delicate liquorice flavour is complemented by cheese and caraway seeds. Serves 4

2 bulbs of fennel
2 tablespoons lemon juice
2 teaspoons caraway seeds
25g (1oz) butter or margarine
100g (4oz) breadcrumbs

200g (7oz) fromage frais
150ml (5fl oz) milk or soya milk
1 teaspoon salt
1 tablespoon chopped fresh parsley

1 Preheat the oven to 200°C/400°F/Gas mark 6. Slice the fennel thinly, reserving the feathery fronds for garnishing. Place the slices in a pan and pour the lemon juice over them. Cover and steam over a medium heat for 5-10 minutes, until the fennel begins to soften.

2 Meanwhile, roast the caraway seeds in a frying pan over a high heat for a few seconds and then crush them slightly. Heat the butter or margarine in a pan and fry the breadcrumbs over a medium heat until slightly browned.

3 Transfer the fennel to a 1.5 litre (2½ pint) baking dish. Beat together the fromage frais, milk, caraway seeds and salt, then pour the mixture over the fennel. Sprinkle the breadcrumbs on top and then the chopped parsley. Cover with foil and bake for 25-30 minutes, until the fennel is tender. Serve hot.

• For a vegan version of this dish, substitute tofu for the fromage frais.

Gobi Masala

Special thanks to Shakti Warwick; her innovative recipe is a feast for the eyes as well as the palate. A whole cauliflower is cooked Indian style to make a deliciously tangy dish. For a milder flavour, reduce the spices or add more yoghurt. Serve with just rice or as part of a larger meal. Serves 4

1 cauliflower
1 fresh green chilli, seeded and finely chopped
½ teaspoon cayenne pepper
¾ teaspoon salt
1 teaspoon grated fresh root ginger
½ teaspoon garam masala plus ½ teaspoon for
  sprinkling
1 teaspoon lemon juice
chopped coriander leaves or parsley, to garnish
Masala paste:
125ml (4fl oz) ghee or oil
2 sticks of celery, finely sliced
1 very small white turnip, finely grated

1 tablespoon grated fresh root ginger
2 tablespoons unsweetened desiccated coconut
50g (2oz) ground almonds
2 tablespoons ground coriander
½ teaspoon cumin seeds
6 whole cloves
8 peppercorns
4 green cardamoms, seeded and husk discarded
pinch of freshly grated nutmeg
2cm (¾in) piece of cinnamon stick
¾ teaspoon salt
4 tablespoons natural yoghurt
1 small tomato, seeded and finely chopped

1 Preheat the oven to 180°C/350°F/Gas mark 4. Wash and dry the cauliflower. Remove the outer leaves.

2 Using a spice grinder or pestle and mortar, grind the chilli, cayenne pepper, ¾ teaspoon salt, 1 teaspoon grated ginger and ½ teaspoon garam masala with the lemon juice to make a paste. Force the paste between the cauliflower florets without breaking them off. Place the cauliflower in a steamer basket and steam for 8-10 minutes, until about three quarters cooked.

3 Meanwhile, make the masala paste. Reserve 2 tablespoons of the ghee or oil. Heat the rest in a frying pan and sauté the celery and turnip. Grind the grated ginger, coconut, almonds, spices and salt together. Stir this mixture into the vegetables. Cook for a moment or two, then slowly add the yoghurt, stirring to prevent it from separating. Stir in the chopped tomato.

4 Place the steamed cauliflower in a casserole dish. Cover the top with half the masala paste, using your hands to push the paste down into the crevices of the vegetable. Drizzle over the reserved ghee or oil. Bake the cauliflower in the oven for 15 minutes, or until the masala is browned and evenly cooked.

5 Pour the remaining masala paste around the cauliflower and bake for another 5 minutes. To serve, sprinkle the cauliflower with the remaining garam masala and garnish with the chopped coriander or parsley.

Vegetable Ragoût
A simple and satisfying winter vegetable dish, retaining all the goodness of the vegetables in the liquid. The addition of dill enhances the flavour of the vegetables. Serve over brown rice with a fresh green salad. Serves 4

3 sticks of celery	1 tablespoon oil or 15g (½oz) butter or margarine
2 or 3 potatoes	6 tomatoes, cut into wedges
2 or 3 carrots	salt and pepper to taste
2 or 3 courgettes	3 tablespoons chopped fresh dill

1 Preheat the oven to 180°C/350°F/Gas mark 4. Chop all the vegetables into large chunks.

2 Heat the oil or butter or margarine in a pan and sauté the celery over a medium heat for about 5 minutes, until it has softened slightly.

3 Place all the chopped vegetables and the tomato wedges in a shallow ovenproof dish, season with salt and pepper and sprinkle with 2 tablespoons of the dill. Pour in enough water to cover the bottom of the dish.

4 Bake in the oven for about 1 hour, until tender, stirring gently from time to time. Add a little more water if it starts to dry out and cover with a lid or foil, if necessary. Serve with the remaining dill sprinkled over the top.

Walnut and Potato Bake
Make sure you buy nuts from a food store with a fast turnover so they are not stale. Look for ones that are not coated with additives. Serve this baked dish with steamed vegetables and a green salad for a simple, yet elegant meal. Serves 4-6

450g (1lb) potatoes, scrubbed but not peeled, then roughly chopped	50ml (2fl oz) milk or soya milk
1 tablespoon butter or oil	50g (2oz) chopped walnuts
225g (8oz) vegetarian cheese, grated, or	tamari to taste
15g (½oz) nutritional yeast flakes	¼ teaspoon paprika
	chopped fresh parsley, to garnish

1 Preheat the oven to 180°C/350°F/Gas mark 4. Steam the potatoes until tender, then mash them and add the butter or oil and grated cheese or yeast flakes. Mix well.

2 Stir in the milk or soya milk, chopped walnuts and tamari to taste. Mix well and transfer to a greased baking dish. Sprinkle with the paprika and bake in the oven for 20 minutes. Garnish with chopped parsley and serve at once.

Baked Stuffed Tomatoes
Rich in vitamins and minerals, tomatoes are a great accompaniment to any meal. If possible, use vine-ripened tomatoes as their flavour is so good. Serve these stuffed tomatoes with a simple green salad or lightly steamed green vegetables for a light lunch or supper, or with Mediterranean Salad (page 98) for a more substantial meal. Serves 4-6

6-8 tomatoes
4 tablespoons oil
1 turnip, grated
50g (2oz) chopped walnuts
1 tablespoon chopped fresh dill or 1 teaspoon
    dried dill weed
1 tablespoon chopped fresh parsley
40g (1½oz) wholewheat breadcrumbs or
    cooked brown rice or other grain
¼ teaspoon pepper
1 teaspoon tamari

1 Preheat the oven to 180°C/350°F/Gas mark 4. Cut a slice off each tomato to make a lid and reserve. Scoop out the pulp using a teaspoon and set aside.

2 Heat half the oil in a pan and cook the turnip until browned. Add the tomato pulp and sauté for 1-2 minutes. Add the chopped walnuts, dill, parsley, breadcrumbs or rice and pepper and sauté for 3 minutes. Stir in the tamari. Spoon the stuffing into the tomatoes. Cover with the reserved 'lids' and sprinkle with the remaining oil.

3 Place the filled tomatoes in a shallow baking dish and add enough water to cover the bottom of the dish. Bake in the oven for 30-40 minutes, then serve hot.

Aubergine Pizzas
Serve hot from the oven as a snack or add a grain dish and salad for a full meal. Serves 4-6

1 large aubergine
4 teaspoons sesame seeds
4 teaspoons dried oregano
4 teaspoons dried basil
salt to taste
150ml (5fl oz) olive oil
2 or 3 large tomatoes, sliced
100g (4oz) vegetarian Cheddar and/or
    mozzarella cheese, grated

1 Preheat the oven to 180°C/350°F/Gas mark 4. Slice the aubergine into 1cm (½in) rounds. Combine the sesame seeds, dried herbs and salt on a plate. Brush the aubergine slices with oil and then dredge in the sesame seed mixture until coated.

2 Place each slice on an oiled baking sheet and top with a slice of tomato and some grated cheese. Bake in the oven for about 30 minutes, or until the aubergine is tender. Serve hot.

• For a vegan version of this dish, substitute 200g (7oz) tofu for the cheese. Slice the tofu and marinate it in a mixture of 3 tablespoons tamari, 3 tablespoons water and 1 tablespoon grated root ginger before adding to the pizzas.

• Sliced olives and/or other toppings may be added before or after baking.

Shepherd's Pie
This is a delicious meal, combining high protein lentils with carbohydrate-rich potato topping. Lentils are rich in iron and one of the easiest pulses to prepare and digest. This pie can be served plain with a simple green salad.
Serves 4-6

300g (10oz) green or brown lentils
700ml (24fl oz) hot water
25g (1oz) butter or margarine
1 green pepper, cored, seeded and chopped
1 red pepper, cored, seeded and chopped
2 carrots, chopped
2 sticks of celery, chopped
1 teaspoon dried mixed herbs (marjoram, thyme, basil)
¼ teaspoon ground mace or nutmeg (optional)
¼ teaspoon cayenne pepper

½ teaspoon salt or 1 teaspoon tamari
2 tomatoes, sliced
chopped fresh parsley
Potato topping:
700g (1lb 9 oz) cooked potatoes
75g (3oz) vegetarian Cheddar cheese, grated (optional)
50g (2oz) butter or margarine
2 tablespoons milk or soya milk
salt and pepper
paprika for sprinkling (optional)

1 Put the lentils in a pan with the hot water. Bring to the boil, half cover and simmer for 30-40 minutes, until the water has been absorbed and the lentils are soft.

2 Preheat the oven to 190°C/375°F/Gas mark 5. Melt the butter or margarine in a frying pan and sauté the peppers, carrots and celery over a medium heat until soft. Mash the cooked lentils and add to the vegetables. Add the herbs, spices and salt or tamari; mix well. Spoon the mixture into a 2 litre (3½ pint) pie dish, arrange the sliced tomatoes on top and sprinkle with the parsley.

3 To make the topping, mash the cooked potatoes with the cheese, butter and milk. Season with salt and pepper. Spoon the potato over the lentil mixture and sprinkle with paprika, if desired. Bake in the oven for about 30 minutes, until the top is golden brown. Serve hot.

• Aduki beans or green or yellow split peas may be used instead of all, or some of, the lentils.
• Make the topping with a mixture of swede, potatoes and parsnip.
• Sprinkle sunflower seeds over the potato, instead of paprika.

Salads
Raw vegetables should be a major component of any healthy diet. Use whatever vegetables are in season. Try not to combine too many different food groups and avoid eating raw vegetables and fruits in the same meal. Leafy green vegetables are a great blessing to humanity; they imbibe the maximum qualities of sunlight and air. They are the lungs and liver of the plants, Nature's storehouse of vitamins and minerals. Green has great power as a healing colour. Eaten fresh and in season, salads add variety, texture and taste to any meal. Serves 4-6

1 cos lettuce, torn into bite-sized pieces
1 bunch of watercress, coarsely chopped

200g (7oz) spinach or chicory, torn into
  bite-sized pieces
salad dressing of your choice (pages 118-120)

Combine the lettuce, watercress and spinach or chicory in a salad bowl. Just before serving, pour over the dressing and toss the salad to coat the leaves in dressing.

• Add any combination of the following: chopped fresh herbs; leafy salad vegetables and/or sprouts; lightly steamed or raw vegetables, such as green beans, broad beans or peas, chopped celery or fennel.

Tri-coloured Salad
This healthy salad platter makes a splendid centrepiece for a festive occasion. The colours are stunning. Serves 4-6

Red – Beetroot salad:
4 raw beetroot, grated
100g (4oz) sunflower seeds, roasted
1 tablespoon chopped fresh thyme or tarragon
250ml (8fl oz) Eggless Mayonnaise (page 120)
  or crème fraîche

Green – Watercress salad:
100g (4oz) walnut pieces
1 bunch of watercress, trimmed
1 green pepper, cored, seeded and sliced
juice of 1 grapefruit
125ml (4fl oz) olive oil
salt and pepper to taste

Orange – Carrot salad, Indian-style:
2 carrots, shredded
1 teaspoon salt (optional)
1 tablespoon raw unsalted peanuts
1 tablespoon oil
½ teaspoon cumin seeds
½ teaspoon black mustard seeds
1 teaspoon sesame seeds
pinch of ground coriander
¼ teaspoon cayenne pepper
1 teaspoon lemon or lime juice
2 tablespoons chopped fresh coriander

1 To make the beetroot salad, combine all the ingredients.

2 To make the watercress salad, heat a heavy frying pan and roast the walnuts over a high heat until browned. Leave to cool, then mix with the watercress and green pepper. In a separate bowl, combine the grapefruit juice, olive oil, salt and pepper and pour over the watercress mixture.

3 To make the carrot salad, place the carrots in a bowl and stir in the salt. Roast the peanuts in the frying pan, stirring constantly until they have turned a darker colour and are giving off a rich aroma. Allow the peanuts to cool and grind them coarsely or crush with a pestle and mortar. Heat the oil in a small pan and roast all the seeds until they 'pop'. Add the ground coriander and cayenne pepper to the seeds and cook for 1 minute, stirring constantly. Stir the mixture into the carrots, along with the peanuts, lemon or lime juice and chopped coriander.

4 Arrange each salad attractively on a large serving platter, keeping them separate.

Mediterranean Salad
Feta cheese and olives add piquancy to this attractive salad and celery gives it a crunchy texture. It will serve four people as a light main course or up to 10 people as a side salad. Serves 4

1-2 tablespoons lemon juice
1-2 tablespoons olive oil
½ teaspoon dried oregano
½ tablespoon fennel seeds, crushed
a few sprigs of fresh coriander, finely chopped
¼ teaspoon salt
pepper to taste .
20 black olives, stoned
100g (4oz) cos lettuce and/or spinach, torn
   into small pieces

300g (10oz) green beans, lightly steamed
2 tomatoes, cut into eight wedges, or
   10 cherry tomatoes
1 cucumber, cut into chunks
3 carrots, cut into thin sticks about
   5cm (2in) long
3 sticks of celery, coarsely chopped
150g (5oz) feta cheese, cubed or crumbled, or
   100g (4oz) sunflower seeds
few sprigs of fresh parsley, to garnish

1 Combine the lemon juice, olive oil, oregano, fennel seeds, coriander, salt and pepper in a small bowl. Set aside to allow the flavours to blend while making the rest of the salad.

2 Mix the olives and vegetables together in a large salad bowl. Add the feta cheese or sunflower seeds and the dressing; mix well. Serve garnished with sprigs of parsley.

Coleslaw
Ideal for when you are eating al fresco, this salad is best made a few hours in advance and kept in the refrigerator to allow the vegetables to absorb the dressing. The red cabbage is not essential, but it adds a lovely colour. Serves 6-8

1 white cabbage
½ a red cabbage (optional)
2 carrots
1 green or red pepper (or ½ of each)
250ml (8fl oz) Eggless Mayonnaise (page 120)

1 tablespoon lemon juice
2 tablespoons caraway seeds, roasted (optional)
1 teaspoon salt
roasted sunflower seeds, to garnish

Shred the white and red cabbages, carrots and pepper, using a food processor or hand grater. Add the mayonnaise, lemon juice and caraway seeds, if using. Season to taste with salt. Transfer to a salad bowl. When ready to serve, sprinkle the roasted sunflower seeds over the top.

• **Fennel Coleslaw:** Replace half the shredded cabbage with shredded fennel and add 1 teaspoon roasted fennel seeds. Use 1 tablespoon walnut oil in the dressing, if you have some. Garnish with fennel fronds and chopped walnuts.

Potato Salad
An essential on a traditional summer picnic, potato salad is easy to prepare. Add a few capers or chopped fresh dill for extra zest. Serves 4-6

- 4-6 potatoes, scrubbed and cubed
- 1 teaspoon salt
- 1 green or red pepper, cored, seeded and diced (optional)

- 1 stick of celery, chopped (optional)
- ½ teaspoon paprika
- 250ml (8fl oz) Eggless Mayonnaise (page 120)

Cook the potatoes in boiling salted water until tender; do not overcook. Drain and leave to cool. When cool, add the other ingredients and toss gently, taking care not to break up the potatoes too much. Serve chilled.

- **German Hot Potato Salad:** Use 1kg (2¼lb) new potatoes, cook them until tender and then slice. While still hot, cover with a little olive oil and lemon juice. Add 1 tablespoon each of chopped fresh mint, parsley and/or dill. Season with salt and pepper. Serve hot.

Sprouts For year-round, fresh, prana-drenched vegetables, nothing beats sprouts. They can be grown anywhere – one of our staff grew a continuous supply in his backpack as he travelled around India for 2 months. However, sprouting is easier on a non-moving window ledge. As sprouts germinate, the fat and starch content decrease while protein, chlorophyll and vitamin C increase. It takes 3-7 days for most sprouts to reach optimum nutritional value.

You can buy sprouting trays at most health food stores, but the easiest method is to use a large glass jar. Soak the pulses, grains or seeds in water overnight. In the morning, secure a piece of cheesecloth or muslin over the opening, drain the water and leave the jar draining at a 45° angle. Rinse the sprouts two or three times a day, draining through the cheesecloth. Mung and Puy lentils take 2-3 days and do not need sun at all. Alfalfa takes 5-7 days – after 3 days, put the jar in a sunny place so that the maximum chlorophyll is formed in the sprouts. Gelatinous seeds, such as cress and flax, do not grow well in a jar. Soak overnight, then place on two or three layers of paper towels on a plate and water two or three times daily. Grains also seem to prefer this method, taking 4-5 days to sprout. They taste very sweet as most of the starch is converted to natural sugars during sprouting. They can be used raw or steamed with a little water for 1-2 minutes.

Sprouts Salad
A few sprouts will add a crunchy texture to any vegetable salad, but they also make an excellent main ingredient for a salad. The ingredients given here are per person – simply multiply the ingredients by the number of diners. Any dressing of your choice (pages 118-120) can be drizzled over the sprouts. Recipe per person

- 25-50g (1-2oz) sprouts
- 25-50g (1-2oz) raw vegetable(s), chopped or shredded

- 1 carrot, grated
- ½ a tomato, sliced (optional)

Place the sprouts in a large bowl and mix in the chopped or shredded vegetables, grated carrot and tomato slices, if using. Serve with a little dressing drizzled over the top.

SATTVIC SWEETS

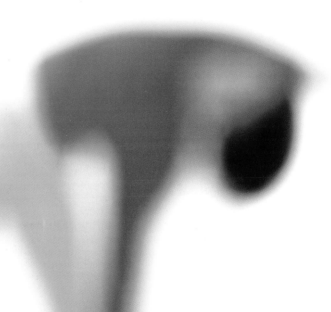

*"Whatever you do, whatever you eat,
whatever you offer in sacrifice, whatever
you give, whatever you practice,
do it as an offering to Me."*

Bhagavad Gita, IX. 27

At the end of any satsang, prasad (blessed food) is distributed. No spiritual event is considered to be complete unless physical food is offered and consumed. The concept of prasad is like the taking of communion in a church. Food, the carrier of love, is first offered to God to be blessed by God and, after this symbolic gesture, is consumed by the participants.

Prasad is food that has been prepared with love by a person who is practising Karma Yoga (selfless service). It is prepared fresh (no more than 2-3 hours before serving), using the best ingredients. It is kept covered and is NEVER tasted before offering. Even a person who is fasting should accept a small piece, as God's Grace should not be refused.

Prasad may be any type of dish, but it is usually sweet, symbolizing the sweetness of God's Grace. Among our Sattvic Sweets, some are traditional prasads and others are more conventional desserts. In a greater sense, any food that is cooked and offered with love may also be seen as prasad.

Raisin Nut Balls

It is the custom at our Christmas parties that everyone makes something. This no-cook recipe is a favourite with the people who think they can't cook, yet want to contribute something. Makes 12

75g (3oz) raisins
50g (2oz) unsalted nuts, such as almonds or hazelnuts

50g (2oz) butter, melted
25g (1oz) shredded unsweetened coconut

1 Chop the raisins in a food processor or blender to a medium fine mixture and transfer to a bowl. Add the nuts to the food processor or blender and chop to a fairly fine mixture. Mix the nuts into the raisins in the bowl. Stir in the melted butter and mix well.

2 Form the mixture into small balls. Spread the coconut on a plate and roll the balls in the coconut until coated. They can be eaten straightaway or chilled before serving.

• Substitute peanut butter or tahini for the melted butter.
• Substitute 2 tablespoons honey for the raisins and double the amount of coconut.
• Add ½ teaspoon grated lemon rind.
• Toast the coconut before rolling the balls in it.
• Roll the balls in carob powder instead of coconut.

Chocolate Truffles

These truffles created by Prema, one of our affiliated teachers in London, are irresistible. They are outrageously sweet, the perfect prasad. Makes 20 large or 40 small

275g (9½oz) icing sugar
75g (3oz) chopped nuts
2 tablespoons cocoa powder
50g (2oz) margarine

1 teaspoon vanilla essence
1-2 tablespoons soya milk
drinking chocolate powder for coating

1 Combine the icing sugar, chopped nuts, cocoa powder, margarine and vanilla essence in a bowl. Slowly add the soya milk; the mixture should be sticky but not runny.

2 Chill until firm, then form the mixture into small balls. Coat with drinking chocolate and keep in the refrigerator or a cool place until ready to serve.

• Ground almonds and almond essence may be substituted for the chopped nuts and vanilla essence.
• Substitute 40g (1½oz) desiccated coconut for the chopped nuts.
• Replace the vanilla essence with 1 teaspoon orange juice and 1 teaspoon finely grated orange rind.

Clockwise from top: Hindustani Halva, Raisin Nut Balls, Chocolate Truffles, Burfi

Hindustani Halva
Semolina is one of the most common prasad ingredients, linked with religious ceremonies such as the 9-night holiday of 'Navaratri' in October. Halva is also often served warm as a breakfast treat. Serves 16-20

200g (7oz) coarse semolina
50g (2oz) unsalted butter
50g (2oz) cashew nut pieces (optional)
200g (7oz) brown sugar

250ml (8fl oz) water
1 teaspoon ground cardamom
50g (2oz) raisins (optional)

1 Toast the semolina in a hot dry frying pan over a high heat for 5 minutes, stirring constantly until it turns light brown and gives off a nutty aroma. Stir in the butter and set aside. If using cashew nuts, roast them in a hot dry pan until slightly browned and set aside.

2 Put the sugar and water in a pan and bring to the boil. Reduce the heat and mix in the semolina, ground cardamom and the raisins and cashew nut pieces, if using. Continue to cook, stirring continuously, until the mixture has thickened.

3 Remove from the heat and spread the mixture evenly on a serving plate. Leave to cool, then score into diamond shapes to make serving easier. Serve with a spoon.

Burfi
This version of the favourite Indian sweet was developed at the Sivananda Yoga Centre in Toronto. Batches were made weekly and delivered to fashionable restaurants and cafés in the city. It's a very rich sweet served in small squares. Use the full cream milk powder available from Indian stores and health food stores, rather than the instant, freeze-dried kind found in supermarkets. Serves 16-20

250g (9oz) butter at room temperature
250ml (8fl oz) clear honey
100g (4oz) walnut pieces

½ teaspoon ground cardamom
250g (9oz) full cream milk powder
a little water or milk, if necessary

1 Break the butter up and melt it in a medium frying pan over a low heat, but do not allow it to cook as it will separate. Remove from the heat, add the honey and mix well.

2 Using a wooden spoon, stir in the nuts, cardamom and milk powder, adding a little water or milk if necessary to dissolve all the powdered milk. The consistency should be firm enough for the spoon to stand up straight in the mixture when you let it go.

3 Spread the mixture in a serving dish and chill until set. Remove from the refrigerator 30 minutes before serving to allow it to come to room temperature. Serve cut into small squares, about 5cm (2in) square.

- Substitute other nuts, such as almonds or pistachios, for the walnuts.
- Add 1-2 saffron strands with the honey.

Sunflower Raisin Cream Pudding *Very sattvic, simple and quick to make, this is a delight for busy people. The pudding can be served on its own or with Raisin or Raspberry Sauce (pages 114 and 115).* Serves 4

150g (5oz) sunflower seeds
100g (4oz) raisins

300ml (10fl oz) water

1 Put the sunflower seeds, raisins and water in a pan and cook the mixture over a medium heat for 15-20 minutes.

2 Transfer the mixture to a food processor or blender and blend to a coarse or a smooth purée. Serve warm or cold.

Banana Berry Delight *A sumptuous pudding that is easy to make. Bananas are believed to increase humility and strawberries to enhance kindness. Chocolate, high in magnesium, is said to help relax the muscles. You can substitute shredded coconut for the chocolate to make this a super healthy 'delight'.* Serves 4-6

3-4 ripe bananas
1 tablespoon lemon juice
125ml (4fl oz) oil
100g (4oz) cooking chocolate, grated

300g (10oz) tofu, steamed
2 tablespoons honey
250g (9oz) ripe strawberries or other berries, sliced

1 Put all the ingredients, except the berries, in a food processor or blender, adding them one at a time and blending before each addition until the mixture is smooth and creamy. Transfer the mixture to a serving dish and stir in the sliced berries. Chill before serving.

Apple Kanten *One of macrobiotic chef Nigel Walker's very sattvic recipes. This traditional macrobiotic dessert is a thick jelly-like custard. It is usually served alone, but is lovely served with Fragrant Fruit Salad (page 145).* Serves 4-6

1.5 litres (2¾ pints) apple juice
3 tablespoons barley malt syrup or rice syrup
2 teaspoons vanilla essence
3 tablespoons finely grated lemon rind

6 tablespoons agar agar flakes
pinch of sea salt
150g (5oz) peeled and chopped eating apple

1 Place all the ingredients, except the apple, in a pan and bring to the boil, stirring. Reduce the heat and simmer for 10-15 minutes, stirring occasionally.

2 Pour the liquid into a serving bowl and leave to cool for about 20 minutes, then gently stir in the chopped apple. Allow to cool, stirring once or twice to ensure the lemon rind is distributed evenly throughout, then chill for 1-2 hours until softly set.

• Substitute orange juice for apple juice, orange rind for lemon, and 1 teaspoon ginger juice (from fresh root ginger) and ¼ teaspoon ground cinnamon for the vanilla essence.
• To make a thicker pudding, add 2 tablespoons arrowroot to a little of the cold apple juice and stir it into the pan while the mixture is being heating.

Chocolate Chick Pea Mousse
Don't be put off by the unusual ingredients in this recipe. It is an incredibly delicious and low-fat mousse. Serve plain or decorated with fruit and/or ice cream. Serves 8

200ml (7fl oz) yoghurt
1 teaspoon bicarbonate of soda
400g (14oz) cooked chick peas, drained [about 200g (7oz) uncooked weight]

75ml (3fl oz) orange juice
200g (7oz) light brown sugar
60g (2½oz) cocoa powder
1 teaspoon baking powder

1 Preheat the oven to 180°C/350°F/Gas mark 4. Oil a 20cm (8in) round cake tin. Mix the yoghurt and bicarbonate of soda together and leave to fizz for 10 minutes.

2 Put the chick peas and orange juice in a food processor or blender (a food processor is best) and blend until smooth. Add the sugar, cocoa and baking powder and blend until smooth. Gently fold the yoghurt mixture into the chick pea mixture.

3 Pour the batter into the prepared tin and bake in the oven for 50 minutes. Remove from the oven and cool in the tin on a wire rack for about 15 minutes. Serve warm or at room temperature.

Apple Crumble
At the Sivananda Yoga Centre in London, we have frequent dinners for students who are doing our Yoga Beginners' Course. On the fifth class they have a practical as well as theoretical introduction to 'Proper Diet'. This is our favourite quick and easy dessert. Serve it on its own or topped with Cornmeal Custard (page 114) or yoghurt. Serves 8-12

Filling:
8 apples, sliced
100g (4oz) raisins (optional)
1 teaspoon ground cinnamon
1 teaspoon lemon juice
½ teaspoon grated fresh root ginger

Topping:
200g (7oz) rolled oats or Granola (page 26)
150g (5oz) wholewheat flour
½ teaspoon salt
100g (4oz) butter or margarine
200ml (7fl oz) honey, corn and barley malt syrup, maple syrup or date syrup

1 Preheat the oven to 190°C/375°F/Gas mark 5. Butter a 20cm (8in) square baking dish. Mix all the filling ingredients together and transfer to the dish.

2 To make the topping, combine the oats or granola, flour and salt. Heat the butter or margarine, add the honey or syrup and mix well. Stir the liquid mixture into the oats. Spoon the topping over the filling. Bake in the oven for about 50 minutes; the filling should be soft but not too runny.

• **Date Banana Crumble:** For the filling, cook 250g (9oz) dates in 250ml (8fl oz) water for 10 minutes. Add 3 mashed ripe bananas and 2 tablespoons lemon juice. Add 100g (4oz) desiccated coconut, if desired. Cook for 5 minutes, then mash the ingredients, leaving the bananas slightly chunky. Make the topping and bake as for the main recipe.

• **Apricot Fig Slice:** Place 350g (12oz) dried apricots and 350g (12oz) dried figs in a pan with 250ml (8 fl oz) orange juice and 1 teaspoon grated orange rind. Cook over a medium heat until soft, then transfer to a food processor or blender and blend until smooth. Spread two thirds of the topping in the baking dish as a base. Spread the purée over it and sprinkle the remaining crumble mixture on top. Bake as for the main recipe.

Pumpkin Pie
A festive favourite at the New York Center's Thanksgiving dinner. Serve the pie with whipped cream, Tofu Whipped Dream or Toasted Nut Dream (page 115). Makes two 20cm (8in) pies

Filling:
1 medium pumpkin
150ml (5fl oz) maple syrup
100g (4oz) silken tofu
¼ teaspoon sea salt
½ teaspoon ground cinnamon
¼ teaspoon ground ginger
pinch of ground mace or freshly grated nutmeg

pinch of ground cloves
1 tablespoon soya flour
Pastry:
300g (10oz) wholewheat pastry flour
1 teaspoon sea salt
25g (1oz) wheatgerm or sesame seeds
160ml (5½fl oz) corn oil
100ml (3½fl oz) chilled sparkling mineral water

1 Preheat the oven to 190°C/375°F/Gas mark 5. Make the filling first. Cut the pumpkin into eighths, remove the seeds and stringy bits. Place the pumpkin in a baking tray, cover with foil and bake in the oven for 45-60 minutes, until soft.

2 Meanwhile, make the pastry. Sift the flour and salt into a large bowl. Stir in the wheatgerm or sesame seeds. Blend in the oil until the pieces are the size of peas. Add the water a tablespoon at a time until the mixture is moist. Knead just enough to hold the dough together. Divide the dough in half and roll into two balls, wrap in greaseproof paper and chill for 30 minutes.

3 Remove the pumpkin from the oven, peel it and purée in a food processor or blender. Add the maple syrup and tofu; blend until smooth. Add the salt, spices and soya flour and mix well.

4 Roll out the dough on a lightly floured surface, use to line two 20cm (8in) flan tins and prick with a fork. Bake in the oven for 8-10 minutes. Increase the temperature to 220°C/425°F/Gas mark 7. Divide the filling between the pastry cases and bake for 45 minutes, until the filling is set.

Tofu Cream Pie
This nourishing pie is the perfect dessert to follow a light main course. Decorate the pie with fresh seasonal fruit, if desired. Serves 8

Crust:
3 tablespoons maple syrup
4 tablespoons oil
4 tablespoons water
150g (5oz) rolled oats
50g (2oz) wholewheat flour
40g (1½oz) sunflower seeds
pinch of salt

Filling:
75g (3oz) soft tofu
1-2 tablespoons tahini
grated rind of 1 lemon
125ml (4fl oz) maple syrup
50ml (2fl oz) oil
50ml (2fl oz) water
pinch of salt

1 Preheat the oven to 200°C/400°F/Gas mark 6 and oil a 23cm (9in) round springform tin.

2 To make the crust, whisk together the maple syrup, oil and water. Add the oats, flour, sunflower seeds and salt. Mix well. Pat the mixture on to the bottom and up the sides of the tin to a depth of about 2.5cm (1in). Bake in the oven for 10-15 minutes, until golden brown. Place the tin on a wire rack and leave to cool. Reduce the oven temperature to 180°C/350°F/Gas mark 4.

3 Put all the filling ingredients in a food processor or blender, purée until smooth, then pour into the baked crust. Bake for 25-30 minutes, until the filling is golden and set. Cool before serving.

Banana Nut Pie
When this recipe was featured in our Yoga Life magazine, it received rave reviews from readers. Bananas are especially beneficial for yoga practitioners, as they are said to increase humility and calmness. Serves 8

Pie shell:
200g (7oz) rolled oats
175g (6oz) wholewheat flour
1 tablespoon honey or date syrup
150ml (5fl oz) oil
200g (7oz) sunflower seeds
water for mixing

Filling:
200g (7oz) cashew nuts
150g (5oz) pitted dates
1 litre (1¾ pints) water
2 tablespoons arrowroot
1 teaspoon grated orange rind
1 teaspoon vanilla essence
2 bananas, plus slices for decoration
200g (7oz) chopped walnuts

1 Preheat the oven to 200°C/400°F/Gas mark 6. Oil a 23cm (9in) loose-bottomed round flan tin. To make the pie shell, mix all the ingredients together, adding a little water to bind them.

2 Spread the mixture in the greased tin, using your hand to spread the mix evenly around the base and sides of the tin. Bake in the oven for 10-15 minutes, until golden. Allow the pie shell to cool completely before removing from the tin.

3 To make the filling, put all the ingredients, except the bananas and chopped walnuts, in a food processor or blender and purée until smooth. Transfer the mixture to a pan and cook over a low heat until it thickens. Remove from the heat and allow to cool.

4 Slice the 2 bananas into the pie shell. Pour the cooled filling on top and decorate with banana slices and the chopped nuts. Chill until set.

Sivananda Cookies
These large, energy-packed cookies are a standard after-class treat at most Sivananada Yoga Centres around the world. They are very nutritious and make a meal in themselves. Makes 12

250g (9oz) rolled oats
100g (4oz) wholewheat flour
150g (5oz) brown sugar
50g (2oz) raisins or sultanas
50g (2oz) raw unsalted peanuts
1½ teaspoons ground cinnamon
1½ teaspoons ground ginger
½ teaspoon freshly grated nutmeg
½ teaspoon baking powder
200ml (7fl oz) oil
about 200ml (7fl oz) water

1 Preheat the oven to 200°C/400°F/Gas mark 6. Oil two or three baking sheets. Combine the dry ingredients in a large mixing bowl, add the oil and mix thoroughly. Stir in enough water to make a firm mixture.

2 Take a spoonful of mixture, about the size of a ping-pong ball. Roll it into a ball, place on one of the oiled baking sheets and flatten to a round about 10cm (4in) in diameter. Repeat to make 12 cookies. Bake in the oven for 12-15 minutes, until golden at the edges. Cool on a wire rack.

• Use sunflower seeds, roughly chopped almonds and/or desiccated coconut instead of, or as well as, the unsalted peanuts.

Gingerbread
The ginger in this warming traditional cake helps to stoke the digestive fire. Gingerbread can be served on its own, or spread with butter, jam or Orange Butter Frosting (page 115), or served with Lemon Sauce (page 114).
Makes 16 squares

125ml (4fl oz) oil
150ml (5fl oz) molasses
200ml (7fl oz) soya milk or natural yoghurt
½ teaspoon salt
450g (1lb) wholewheat flour

⅓ teaspoon ground cloves
1½ teaspoons bicarbonate of soda
⅔ teaspoon ground ginger
1 teaspoon ground cinnamon

1 Preheat the oven to 180°C/350°F/Gas mark 4. Lightly oil a 20cm (8in) square cake tin.

2 Mix the oil, molasses, soya milk or yoghurt in a large mixing bowl. In a separate bowl, mix the dry ingredients and sift them into the molasses mixture, stirring in the bran that remains in the sieve. Mix thoroughly.

3 Pour into the prepared tin and bake in the oven for 40 minutes. The cake is ready when a fine skewer inserted into the centre comes out clean. Leave to cool in the tin. Turn out and cut into squares to serve.

Carob Nut Brownies
Although it is often used as a chocolate substitute, carob has its own very distinctive taste. It has a very low fat content and is rich in vitamins and minerals. These brownies may be served plain or iced with Carob Frosting (page 115). Makes 24

150ml (5fl oz) oil or melted butter
250ml (8fl oz) honey or date syrup
500ml (18fl oz) water
500g (1lb 2oz) wholewheat flour
150g (5oz) milk powder

200g (7oz) carob powder
½ teaspoon salt
2 teaspoons baking powder
250g (9oz) walnut pieces

1 Preheat the oven to 180°C/350°F/Gas mark 4. Oil a 20 x 30cm (8 x 12in) baking tin.

2 Mix the oil or butter, honey or date syrup and water in a large mixing bowl. In a separate bowl, mix the flour, milk powder, carob powder, salt and baking powder. Sift them into the honey mixture, stirring in the bran that remains in the sieve. The consistency should be fairly runny; add more water if necessary. Stir in the walnut pieces.

3 Pour the batter into the tin and bake in the oven for 30 minutes. Leave to cool in the tin, then turn out and cut into squares.

• **Wheatgerm Brownies:** Reduce the amount of honey or date syrup to 150ml (5fl oz) and add 50ml (2fl oz) molasses and 2 teaspoons vanilla essence. Omit the carob powder and reduce the quantity of walnut pieces to 200g (7oz). Stir 150g (5oz) raisins and 20g (¾oz) lightly toasted wheatgerm into the mixture with the walnut pieces.

Apple Sauce Spice Cake
Cloves, cinnamon and nutmeg give this cake a wonderful flavour, making it perfect for an afternoon snack or a festive cake at Christmas time. The cake can be served plain or covered with Butter Frosting (page 115). Serves 6-10

3 eating apples
125ml (4fl oz) water
100g (4oz) clear honey or barley malt syrup
50g (2oz) butter, melted, or 4 tablespoons oil
300g (10oz) wholewheat flour
1 teaspoon bicarbonate of soda
½ teaspoon sea salt

1 teaspoon ground cinnamon
½ teaspoon ground cloves
½ teaspoon ground allspice
½ teaspoon freshly grated nutmeg
¼ teaspoon ground ginger
150g (5oz) chopped nuts (unroasted and unsalted) or raisins

1 Preheat the oven to 190°C/375°F/Gas mark 5. Grease and flour a 900g (2lb) loaf tin.

2 Peel the apples if they are not organic. Quarter them, remove the cores and cut into thin slices. Place in a pan with the water, cover and simmer over a low heat for about 10 minutes, until the apples are soft. Remove from the heat and mash to a smooth sauce.

3 Mix the apple sauce, honey or barley malt syrup and melted butter or oil in a large mixing bowl until smooth. In a separate bowl, mix the flour, bicarbonate of soda, salt and spices, then sift into the apple sauce mixture, stirring in the bran that remains in the sieve. Stir until blended but do not beat. Add the nuts or raisins. Pour into the loaf tin and bake in the oven for 40-50 minutes, or until firm to the touch. Leave to cool in the tin before slicing and serving.

Peanut Butter Carob Cake
Serves 8-10

Peanut butter mixture:
75g (3oz) butter
300g (10oz) honey or other sweetener
2 teaspoons vanilla essence
125ml (4fl oz) natural yoghurt
3 tablespoons milk
350g (12oz) wholewheat flour
2 teaspoons baking powder

pinch of salt
150g (5oz) peanut butter
Carob mixture:
2 tablespoons milk
½ teaspoon honey
1 tablespoon carob powder
¼ teaspoon ground cinnamon

1 Preheat the oven to 190°C/375°F/Gas mark 5. Lightly oil a 20cm (8 in) square cake tin.

2 To make the peanut butter mixture, cream the butter and honey or other sweetener in a large mixing bowl, then add the vanilla essence, yoghurt and milk and mix well. Sift the flour, baking powder and salt into the butter mixture, stirring in the bran that remains in the sieve, and mix well. Transfer 200g (7oz) of this mixture to a separate bowl and set aside for the carob mixture. Stir the peanut butter into the remaining mixture and spoon it into the prepared cake tin.

3 To make the carob mixture, add the 2 tablespoons milk, ½ teaspoon honey, the carob powder and cinnamon to the reserved mixture. Stir the carob mixture into the cake mixture in the tin in a zig-zag pattern. Level the surface and bake in the oven for about 30 minutes, until firm to the touch. Cool in the tin for a few minutes, cut into squares and serve warm or cool.

Tofu Prune Cake
When we tested this recipe at our London Centre, the demand for copies of the recipe reached an all-time high. Dates or other dried fruits may be substituted for the prunes. Serve with fresh fruit, if desired. Serves 12

250ml (8fl oz) oil
450g (1lb) firm tofu
350g (12oz) soft brown sugar
rind and juice of 2 lemons

550g (1¼lb) self-raising flour
1 teaspoon baking powder
450g (1lb) prunes, chopped
Orange or Lemon Butter Frosting (page 115)

1 Preheat the oven to 180°C/350°F/Gas mark 4. Grease a 24cm (9½in) cake tin and line the base with baking parchment.

2 Put the oil, tofu, sugar and lemon juice in a food processor or blender and blend until creamy and smooth. Transfer to a mixing bowl and sift in the flour and baking powder, then stir in the lemon rind and prunes.

3 Spoon the mixture into the prepared cake tin and bake in the oven for 1-1¼ hours, until a fine skewer inserted into the centre comes out clean. Leave to cool in the tin, then turn out and spread with frosting before serving.

Passion Cake
This cake is a favourite at our Easter retreats. We take over a large country house and immerse ourselves in yoga practice for five days, with periodic breaks for a game of football, a talent show or a bit of sweetness such as this cake. Serves 8-12

250g (9oz) wholewheat flour
2 teaspoons baking powder
1 teaspoon ground mixed spice
2 teaspoons ground cinnamon
3 tablespoons soya flour
6 tablespoons water
175g (6oz) soft brown sugar
50g (2oz) pecan nuts or walnuts, chopped
1 large very ripe banana
50g (2oz) dried figs, chopped
25g (1oz) sultanas

1 tablespoon lime marmalade
150g (5oz) carrots, finely grated
175ml (6fl oz) oil
Icing:
200g (7oz) creamed coconut
about 75ml (3fl oz) hot water
grated rind of ½ an orange
3-4 tablespoons icing sugar
3 tablespoons orange juice
100g (4oz) lightly toasted desiccated coconut

1 Preheat the oven to 190°C/375°F/Gas mark 5. Grease and base line a 20cm (8in) round cake tin. Combine the wholewheat flour, baking powder and spices in a large mixing bowl. Mix the soya flour with the water and stir into the bowl with the sugar and nuts. Mash the banana and add it with the figs, sultanas, marmalade, carrots and oil. Mix thoroughly.

2 Transfer the mixture to the prepared tin and level the top. Bake in the oven for 40-50 minutes, or until firm to the touch. Leave to cool in the tin. Using a round-bladed knife, ease the sides of the cake away from the tin, then carefully turn out and peel off the lining paper.

3 To make the icing, mash the creamed coconut in a bowl with some of the hot water, using a fork, then beat in the orange rind, icing sugar and orange juice with enough hot water to give the mixture a smooth consistency for spreading on the top and sides of the cake. Sprinkle evenly with the toasted desiccated coconut.

Rich Tofu Fruit Cake
No baking powder is needed for Nigel Walker's scrumptious cake as the tofu and breadcrumbs make it light. Serves 8-12

1 orange
½ a lemon
200g (7oz) wholewheat breadcrumbs
200g (7oz) currants
150g (5oz) sultanas
1 tablespoon mugi miso
4 tablespoons apple juice concentrate
2 tablespoons wholewheat flour
250g (9oz) tofu, mashed
3 tablespoons barley malt syrup

2 eating apples, grated
150g (5oz) walnuts, lightly roasted
2 tablespoons cold pressed corn oil
75g (3oz) rolled oats
orange juice (optional)
1 teaspoon freshly grated nutmeg
3 teaspoons ground cinnamon
2 teaspoons ground ginger
100g (4oz) creamed coconut, shredded and dissolved in 300ml (10fl oz) water

1 Preheat the oven to 160°C/325°F/Gas mark 3. Line a 23cm (9in) cake tin with greaseproof paper and oil it. Peel the orange and lemon. Slice the peel finely. Chop the flesh, removing pips.

2 Combine all the ingredients with a wooden spoon, adding more juice or rolled oats to achieve a consistency like thick wet mud. Turn into the cake tin, cover with foil and bake in the oven for 3 hours, or until firm to the touch. Leave to cool on a wire rack for several hours before turning out.

Cornmeal Custard
This custard makes a delicious change from the traditional type made with cornflour. Serves 4

1 litre (1¾ pints) milk or soya milk
2 tablespoons clear honey or maple syrup
handful of sultanas (optional)

½ teaspoon vanilla essence
3 tablespoons coarse cornmeal

Place the milk, honey or maple syrup, sultanas and vanilla essence in a pan and bring to the boil. Whisk in the cornmeal slowly and cook until it thickens, whisking frequently. Serve hot.

Ginger and Lemon Sauce
Serves 4

zest and juice of ½ a lemon
4 tablespoons apple juice

25g (1oz) demerara sugar
½ teaspoon ground ginger

Mix all the ingredients in a pan and bring to the boil slowly, stirring constantly. Simmer for about 5 minutes, then serve hot.

• Omit the ground ginger to make a tangy lemon sauce.

Raisin Sauce
Raisins are said to remedy an over-critical nature, bringing out tenderness. Serves 4

200g (7oz) raisins
300-400ml (10-14fl oz) water

about 1 teaspoon vanilla essence
about 1 teaspoon ground cinnamon

Put the raisins in a pan with enough of the water to cover them. Bring to the boil and simmer for 20 minutes. Transfer to a blender and blend to a coarse or a smooth purée. If it is too thick, add more water. Add vanilla essence and cinnamon to taste. Reheat until hot or serve warm.

Raspberry Sauce *Raspberries are said to enhance kindness. If you like, strawberries can be used instead; they may not need sweetening.* Serves 4

150g (5oz) fresh raspberries

about 2 tablespoons honey or soft brown sugar

Purée the raspberries in a food processor or blender. Add honey or soft brown sugar to taste and serve hot.

Butter Frosting *Use full cream milk powder, available from Indian stores and health food stores.* Enough for 1 cake

225g (8oz) butter at room temperature
125ml (4fl oz) honey or other sweetener
2 tablespoons milk

½ tablespoon vanilla essence
100g (4oz) full cream milk powder

Whip the butter in a food processor or blender. Add the remaining ingredients one at a time, beating after each addition. Leave to cool before using.

- **Lemon or Orange Butter Frosting:** Omit the milk and vanilla essence and add the juice of 2 lemons or 3 oranges. Sprinkle with a little grated rind, if desired.
- **Carob Frosting:** Use 50g (2oz) milk powder and add 50g (2oz) carob powder.

Tofu Whipped Dream *Suitable for vegans, this dreamy topping can be used as a cake icing or on desserts.* Serves 4-6

225g (8oz) tofu, steamed for 2-3 minutes
3 tablespoons honey, maple syrup or apple juice concentrate

1 teaspoon vanilla essence
water or fruit juice, if necessary

Place the tofu, honey, maple syrup or apple juice concentrate and vanilla essence in a food processor or blender and blend until the mixture is like whipped cream. Add water or fruit juice to thin it, if desired. Use straight away or chill overnight before serving.

- Use rose water or orange flower water instead of vanilla essence.
- Add the grated rind of 1 orange or lemon.
- Add 25g (1oz) ground almonds and a few drops of almond essence.

Toasted Nut Dream *Serve this nut cream as a topping for fruit salads, pies or any other desserts.* Serves 4-6

250g (9oz) hazelnuts
150ml (5fl oz) soya milk
1 teaspoon lemon juice

1-2 tablespoons honey
pinch of salt

Roast the hazelnuts in a hot dry frying pan over a high heat until lightly browned. Leave to cool. Put all the ingredients in a food processor or blender and blend until creamy.

- Substitute almonds for the hazelnuts and add a few drops of vanilla essence.
- Substitute walnuts for the hazelnuts and use maple syrup instead of honey.

FINISHING TOUCHES

*"Serve, Love, Give, Purify,
Meditate, Realize."*

Swami Sivananda

Traditionally it is suggested that food be offered with love to all guests, even if they have arrived uninvited. The wise person graciously receives any guest with the words "Food is ready". The best food should be given in abundance with faith and devotion, courtesy and humility. Then the yogic principle that 'the guest is GOD' will become a living, breathing reality.

Through this practice of service, love for humanity develops. From love, one learns to give of oneself. Only then are we able to purify the mind completely and prepare it to meditate and realize the peace and happiness that lie within.

While most vegetables, grains and proteins taste good by themselves, a simple sauce or salad dressing can help to light the digestive fire. It is this digestive fire that 'cooks' the food within the body, transforming it into blood, flesh and bone. Adding a finishing touch such as a dressing or sauce can turn a simple dish into a special meal.

Seed Toppings Seed toppings make a lovely garnish to sprinkle over salads, vegetables, pulses or grains. Seeds can be rinsed before roasting, if desired; it makes them expand and helps to prevent them from burning.

Pumpkin Seed and Wakame Topping: Preheat the oven to 180°C/350°F/Gas mark 4. Roast a handful of pumpkin seeds in a dry frying pan over a high heat until they 'pop'. Place 4-5 strips of wakame on a baking sheet and bake in the oven for 5-10 minutes, until dry. Grind the seaweed and pumpkin seeds together, making the mixture as coarse or as fine as you like.

Tamari and Sunflower Seeds: Roast a handful of sunflower seeds in a hot dry frying pan over a high heat until they are golden. Turn off the heat and add a few drops of tamari to coat the seeds.

Gomasio: This is a tasty way to reduce salt consumption. Roast a handful of sesame seeds in a hot dry frying pan over a high heat until they give off a pleasant aroma. Combine 1 part rock salt or coarse sea salt to 15 parts sesame seeds and grind with a pestle and mortar. It is worth making a good amount of this mixture at a time as it stores well.

Basic Salad Dressing

There is no limit to the ingredients that can be used in salad dressings, but as vinegar is not used in a yogic diet they are usually made with fresh citrus juices. Freshly squeezed grapefruit is the least acid-forming of all citrus fruits and makes a lovely change from lemon. Or, try orange juice instead of, or in combination with, the lemon juice. Try to use cold-pressed oils. Olive oil is always a treat in a salad dressing; use it alone or in combination with other oils. Yoghurt, tofu and lecithin are expanders and are used to give dressings a creamy texture. Tofu should be steamed for 2-3 minutes before using it in the dressings. Use any herbs you wish, such as basil, rosemary, thyme, mint or dill, or seeds such as caraway or cumin. Some people also like to blend in 1 tablespoon honey. At the Sivananda Yoga Retreat in the Bahamas, we often blend the salad left from the previous meal with a little lemon juice, tamari and dill or other herbs. It never comes out the same twice, is always good, and guests beg for the 'special green salad dressing' recipe. Serves 4-6

125ml (4fl oz) oil
4 tablespoons lemon juice

1 tablespoon tamari or 1 teaspoon sea salt

Place all the ingredients in a bowl or screw-top jar and whisk together or shake until mixed.

• **French Dressing:** Use salt not tamari. Blend the ingredients in a blender with 2 chopped tomatoes, 1 tablespoon fresh dill or $\frac{1}{2}$ teaspoon dried dill weed and $\frac{1}{4}$ teaspoon pepper.
• Add any chopped fresh herbs or seeds such as caraway or cumin.
• Use freshly squeezed grapefruit or orange juice instead of the lemon juice (or a mixture of all three).

Sunflower Seed Dressing
This is the current favourite at the London Centre. Sunflower seeds, which are rich in B vitamins, give a creaminess to this dressing and stop the ingredients from separating. Serves 4-6

5 tablespoons oil
2 tablespoons lemon juice
about 50g (2oz) sunflower seeds

1 tablespoon tamari or 1 teaspoon salt
5 tablespoons water

Put all the ingredients in a blender and blend until smooth. Add more water or more sunflower seeds, depending on how thick you want the dressing to be.

• Use toasted sesame seed oil and add 1cm (½in) piece of fresh root ginger, peeled and grated.
• Replace the sunflower seeds with pumpkin seeds or use a mixture of the two.

Tahini Mint Dressing
The tahini gives this dressing a hint of Middle Eastern flavours. It is particularly good drizzled over salad leaves or fruit. Tahini has a very high oil content, so no extra oil is needed. Makes 250ml (8fl oz)

75g (3oz) tahini
juice of 1 lemon
dash of tamari

125ml (4fl oz) water
1 tablespoon chopped fresh mint

Mix all the ingredients together in a blender or whisk them in a bowl. Thin the dressing with a little more water, if necessary.

• Use 3 tablespoons peanut butter instead of tahini and omit the mint.
• For a lovely topping for fruit salads, omit the tamari and use apple juice instead of water. Add a little honey, if desired.
• Omit the water and serve it as a party dip with vegetable crudités, crisps or crackers.

Creamy Italian Dressing
This rich, thick creamy dressing is excellent for salads. Alternatively, it can be used as a dressing for pasta. Serves 4-6

100g (4oz) chick peas, cooked
75ml (3fl oz) olive oil
1 teaspoon dried oregano
pinch of dried dill weed

3 tablespoons lemon juice
1 teaspoon salt
½ teaspoon pepper

Put the chick peas in a food processor or blender and blend until smooth. Add all the remaining ingredients and blend again until smooth. If necessary, thin with water or more oil to the desired consistency. Chill before serving.

Seeded Yoghurt Dressing

Caraway seeds – excellent for helping the digestion – give this oil-free dressing a sweet and spicy taste. Fennel, anise or cumin seeds can be used instead of caraway. Makes 250ml (8fl oz)

2 tablespoons sesame seeds
1 teaspoon caraway seeds
200ml (7fl oz) yoghurt

½ teaspoon mustard powder
1 tablespoon lemon juice
½ teaspoon salt

Roast the seeds in a hot dry frying pan over a high heat until they begin to smell aromatic. Crush them slightly and blend with the other ingredients in a blender or whisk them in a bowl. Thin with a little water, if necessary.

• For a richer dressing, substitute soured cream for all or part of the yoghurt.
• For a vegan version, replace the yoghurt with 200g (7oz) silken tofu, steamed for 2-3 minutes and crumbled.

Eggless Mayonnaise

Use as a healthy alternative to commercial salad cream. The lecithin is used as an emulsifier instead of eggs, but you can make it without, if preferred. Makes 250ml (8fl oz)

150ml (5fl oz) soya milk
75ml (3fl oz) oil
2 tablespoons lemon juice
½ teaspoon salt or tamari

¼ teaspoon mustard powder
1 tablespoon liquid lecithin or 1 teaspoon lecithin granules (optional)

Place all the ingredients in a blender and blend until smooth. Leave the mayonnaise to set for about 1 hour before using.

• Add ½ teaspoon curry powder and ¼ teaspoon turmeric.
• Add ½ a bunch of parsley, chopped.
• Blend in 2 tablespoons tahini.
• For a thicker mayonnaise, reduce the oil to 2 tablespoons and blend in 150g (5oz) tofu, steamed for 2-3 minutes and crumbled.
• For dill mayonnaise, mix in a small bunch of fresh dill, chopped, or 1 teaspoon dried dill weed, and 1 tablespoon tomato purée or 2 chopped tomatoes.

Cashew Nut Gravy

With their high protein and mineral content, cashew nuts add a creamy richness to steamed vegetables or grains, increasing the nutritional value of a meal. Walnuts can be substituted, if preferred. Serves 6

50g (2oz) raw cashew nuts
1 tablespoon arrowroot

200ml (7fl oz) vegetable stock or water, plus extra if necessary
1 teaspoon tamari

Roast the cashew nuts in a hot dry frying pan over a high heat until lightly browned. Put the nuts, arrowroot and stock or water in a food processor or blender and blend until smooth. Pour into a pan and heat over a medium heat for 3-5 minutes, until thickened, stirring constantly. Dilute with additional vegetable stock or water, if desired. Stir in the tamari and serve hot.

Rich Brown Gravy

Butter or margarine will give the best flavour but corn, safflower or other low-cholesterol oils can be used. Any herbs, fresh or dried, can be added to this gravy: basil is especially suggested; sage, thyme and savory will give a very traditional gravy; oregano, marjoram or rosemary, a more Italian flavour. Wholewheat flour or chick pea flour (also known as besan or gram flour) can be used instead of arrowroot. Chick pea flour adds a lovely nutty flavour. Makes 350ml (12fl oz)

25g (1oz) butter or margarine
3 tablespoons arrowroot
300ml (10fl oz) water
chopped fresh herbs or dried herbs to taste

2 tablespoons tamari
1 teaspoon tomato purée (optional)
pepper to taste

Melt the butter or margarine in a pan over a medium heat. Stir in the arrowroot and gradually whisk in the water, stirring continuously to ensure a smooth, lump-free sauce. If using dried herbs, add them with the water. Bring to simmering point and simmer until the gravy is thick. Add the tamari and tomato purée and fresh herbs, if using. Season with pepper.

• For a vegetable gravy, sauté 75-100g (3-4oz) grated vegetables (turnip, cabbage and/or carrots) in the butter or margarine before adding the arrowroot. To give the gravy extra 'zing', add 1 tablespoon grated fresh root ginger. This is particularly good served with Kasha Varnishkas (page 62) or other grain dishes.
• Replace 4 tablespoons of the water with apple or unsweetened grape juice and add 1 teaspoon lemon juice just before serving.
• Omit the tomato purée and add 2 teaspoons nutritional yeast flakes, a pinch of dried sage and thyme and 2 tablespoons lemon juice.
• Remove from the heat and stir in 50g (2oz) grated cheese, or 2 tablespoons miso, or 125ml (4fl oz) tahini.
• Add a pinch of ground cumin or paprika for a more piquant gravy.

Miso Sesame Sauce

Miso is rich in vitamin B12 and has a warming and toning effect on the system, while sesame seeds are rich in calcium. Serve this sauce over steamed kale or other green vegetables for a balanced, appetizing dish. Serves 4

150g (5oz) butter or margarine
75g (3oz) sesame seeds

2 teaspoons white miso

Melt the butter or margarine in a small pan. Roast the sesame seeds in a hot dry frying pan over a high heat until golden brown, stirring constantly to prevent them from burning. Remove from the heat. Add them to the melted butter and stir in the miso. Serve at once.

• Add 1-2 tablespoons chopped fresh parsley or coriander to the melted butter and sauté briefly before adding the sesame seeds.
• Use half butter and half sesame oil.
• Add 1 teaspoon tamari with the miso.

No-cheese Sauce

This is a vegan delight over steamed vegetables, grains or pulses. Serves 6-8

60g (2½oz) margarine
60g (2½oz) wholewheat flour
750ml (1¼ pints) soya milk
½ teaspoon mustard powder

15g (½oz) nutritional yeast flakes
¼ teaspoon freshly grated nutmeg (optional)
salt and pepper

Melt the margarine in a pan, add the flour and cook over a low heat for 1-2 minutes. Whisk in the soya milk and cook until thickened. Add the mustard, yeast flakes and nutmeg, if using. Season to taste with salt and pepper.

Tomato Sauce

This thick, chunky sauce can be served on vegetables, pasta or grains. If possible, use deep red, juicy tomatoes and make the sauce in advance so it can stand for a few hours to bring out the flavour. Makes 500ml (18fl oz)

2 tablespoons olive oil
2 sticks of celery, finely chopped
1 carrot, grated
1 bay leaf
350g (12oz) fresh or canned tomatoes, chopped

150ml (5fl oz) tomato purée
2 tablespoons chopped fresh oregano or basil
   or 1 tablespoon dried herbs
1 teaspoon salt
pinch of pepper

Heat the oil in a frying pan and sauté the celery over a medium heat until soft. Add the carrot, bay leaf, tomatoes and tomato purée and simmer for 45 minutes. Add the herbs and season with salt and pepper. Serve as a chunky sauce or purée in a food processor or blender for smooth sauce.

• To use in lasagne, substitute 450g (1lb) mixed diced vegetables (courgette, green pepper, carrot) for the celery and carrot.

• To use as a pizza topping, substitute 350g (12oz) red, yellow and/or green peppers, cored, seeded and chopped, for the celery. Add a pinch of cayenne pepper, if desired.

Ginger Sauce

A light, spicy sauce for steamed vegetables, noodles or tofu. The healing properties of ginger are legion and it plays a very strong part in the yogic diet, as it stimulates the digestion without having a similarly stimulating effect on the mind. It is excellent for warming the system, improving blood circulation and helping to cure colds and flu. Serves 4

200ml (7fl oz) water
2 tablespoons tamari
2½ tablespoons molasses or barley malt syrup
1½ teaspoons cornflour or arrowroot

1½ tablespoons water
1 teaspoon grated fresh root ginger
1 tablespoon apple juice or white grape juice
2 teaspoons lemon juice

1 Heat the water in a pan. Add the tamari and the molasses or barley malt syrup and simmer over a medium heat for about 5 minutes.

2 Dissolve the cornflour or arrowroot in the 1½ tablespoons water, add to the pan and bring to the boil. Add the grated ginger and apple or grape juice and cook for another 2 minutes. Remove from the heat and stir in the lemon juice.

Salsa

This quick party dip is lightly spiced and perfect for serving with crudités, wholemeal crackers or pitta bread. Serves 6

1 tablespoon oil
½ teaspoon celery seeds
1 teaspoon cumin seeds
1 small turnip, grated
1 fresh green chilli, seeded and chopped
500g (1lb 2oz) fresh tomatoes, finely chopped

½ teaspoon ground coriander
½ teaspoon cayenne pepper
1 tablespoon chopped fresh oregano or
    ½ teaspoon dried oregano
1 teaspoon salt

Heat the oil in a heavy pan and roast the celery and cumin seeds over a high heat until they 'pop'. Add the turnip and chilli and sauté over a medium heat for 5 minutes. Transfer to a food processor or blender and purée until smooth. Pour into a bowl and stir in the chopped tomatoes, spices, oregano and salt. Allow to set and serve at room temperature.

Orange Dill Sauce

The lime and ginger give this sauce a lovely tang, making it a refreshing topping for steamed vegetables. Serves 4-6

2cm (¾in) piece of fresh root ginger, peeled
    and chopped
zest and juice of 1 orange
zest and juice of 1 lime
1 teaspoon salt
pepper

200ml (7fl oz) water
2 tablespoons arrowroot
2 tablespoons finely chopped fresh dill or
    1 tablespoon dried dill weed
40g (1½oz) butter or margarine

1 Put all the ingredients, except the dill and butter or margarine, in a food processor or blender and blend until smooth. Stir in the dill.

2 Melt the butter or margarine in a pan, add the mixture and cook over a medium heat for 3-4 minutes until slightly thickened. Serve warm.

Gado Gado

This traditional Indonesian sauce adds a piquant flavour to the simplest of dishes, such as lightly steamed carrots, green beans, asparagus, broccoli and cauliflower, or grains. Use good quality peanut butter. Serves 4-6

1½ tablespoons oil
½ a stick of celery or ¼ green pepper, cored,
    seeded and diced
1 tablespoon chopped fresh root ginger
pinch of curry powder, ground cumin or cayenne
    pepper (optional)

150g (5oz) crunchy peanut butter
about 250ml (8fl oz) boiling water
50g (2oz) desiccated coconut
2 tablespoons tamari
1½ teaspoons honey
juice of ½ a lemon

1 Heat the oil in a wok or frying pan. Add the diced celery or green pepper, ginger and curry powder, cumin or cayenne pepper, if using. Sauté over a low heat for about 5 minutes, until soft. Add the peanut butter, stirring to prevent it from scorching. When the mixture is bubbling, stir in enough boiling water to give it the consistency of thin cream.

2 Bring back to the boil over a high heat. Lower the heat and add the coconut and tamari. Simmer for about 10 minutes, until the oil rises to the top of the sauce. Remove from the heat and stir in the honey and lemon juice.

Cranberry Sauce
High in vitamin C, the tart flavour of cranberries makes them the ideal accompaniment to rich dishes. This sauce is one of the traditions of Thanksgiving or Christmas dinner, but can be served at any time.
Serves 4-6

75g (3oz) dried dates, chopped
4 tablespoons water
375g (13oz) raw cranberries
2 cinnamon sticks, each 2.5cm (1in) long

5 cloves
½ an orange, thinly sliced with the rind on
4 tablespoons honey

1 Place the dates in a pan with the water. Bring to the boil, then remove from the heat and leave to stand for an hour or so.

2 Place the cranberries in a heavy pan with the cinnamon, cloves, orange slices, dates and the water. Cook uncovered over a medium heat until thick, then remove from the heat and allow to cool. Add the honey and allow to set before serving.

Coconut Chutney
This lovely chutney is simple to prepare. Its spicy tang is cooled by the coconut, making it a suitable accompaniment for any meal. In South India, it is traditionally served with Dosas (page 28) for breakfast. Add a bunch of chopped fresh coriander for a green chutney. Serves 4-6

100g (4oz) desiccated coconut
3 tablespoons chopped curry leaves
1 green chilli, seeded and chopped
1cm (½in) piece fresh root ginger, peeled and
  grated
1 carrot, grated

1 tablespoon ghee
1 teaspoon black mustard seeds
1 tablespoon lemon juice
1-2 teaspoons paprika
1 teaspoon salt

1 Soak the coconut in just enough water to cover for 15-20 minutes, then squeeze out the liquid. Add the chopped curry leaves, green chilli, ginger and carrot. Toss the mixture with your hands until everything is well mixed.

2 Heat the ghee in a frying pan and roast the mustard seeds over a high heat until they 'pop'. Add the ghee and mustard seeds to the coconut mixture and mix well, then stir in the lemon juice, paprika and salt.

Mint Chutney
A traditional accompaniment for Indian snacks. Try it with any type of savoury dish or spread on sandwiches. Serves 4-6

4-6 cashew nuts
4cm (1½in) piece of fresh root ginger, peeled
  and grated
1 green pepper, cored, seeded and chopped
  (optional)

1 tablespoon chopped fresh mint
1 teaspoon lemon juice
1 teaspoon salt
½ teaspoon ground coriander
4 tablespoons natural yoghurt (optional)

Put the cashew nuts, ginger, green pepper, if using, and mint in a food processor or blender and blend to a fine pulp. Add the rest of the ingredients and mix thoroughly. Allow the chutney to set for at least 1 hour before serving.

Miso Nut Spread
This is a healthy yeast-free alternative to the commercial yeast extract spreads. It can be used as a topping or as a spread on bread or crackers. Add a little salad for an unusual sandwich filling. Serves 4-6

2 tablespoons hazelnuts or almonds
2 tablespoons light miso

1 tablespoon water

Roast the nuts in a hot dry frying pan over a high heat until lightly browned. Place them in a blender with the miso and water. Blend together until smooth.

- Substitute any nut butter or tahini for the nuts.
- Vary the type of miso.

Olive Spread
This attractive spread serves four as a sandwich stuffing or many more as a topping on crackers for party nibbles. Spread on wholewheat bread and garnished with salad cress or parsley sprigs, it makes a tasty picnic or lunch snack. Serves 4-6

20 green olives stuffed with pimento
3 tablespoons walnut pieces

½ a red pepper, cored, seeded and chopped
2 tablespoons oil

Put all the ingredients in a blender and blend to a coarse purée. Alternatively, chop the ingredients very finely. Allow to set for about 1 hour before serving.

- For a green spread, omit the walnuts and red pepper. Halve the amount of oil and blend in 4 tablespoons chopped fresh parsley and 2 tablespoons tahini.

Cottage Cheese Topping
This makes a tasty topping for steamed vegetables and new or baked potatoes, or it can be spread on toast for a nutritious breakfast or a light lunch dish. Serves 4-6

1 teaspoon lemon juice
1 tablespoon raw wheatgerm
3 tablespoons cottage cheese

1 tablespoon seasame oil
250ml (8fl oz) natural yoghurt
  or soured cream

Mix all the ingredients together in a bowl and serve straight away.

YOGIC
FEASTS

"You are an ocean of Bliss, an embodiment of Joy. You are in reality the Lord of the three worlds. If you give up egoism, selfishness and greed, you will realize God here and now. God has given you faculties and potentialities, so rise up. Keep your faculties bright and brilliant by taking a pure diet."

Swami Sivananda

OM
Anna Poorne Sadha Poorne
Shankara Prana Vallabhe
Jnana Vairagya Siddyartham
Bhiksham Dhehee Cha Parvati

Divine Mother, who comes to out table as food,
You are the endlessly bountiful, benefactress of all.
Please grant us wisdom, dispassion, strength and
O Mother, give us health.

OM
Mata Me Parvati Devi
Pita Devo Mahashwara
Bandhava Siva Bhaktascha
Swadesho Bhuvana Trayam

Mother Nature is my Mother Divine
The Lord of the Universe is my Father
All the people of the world are my friends and relatives.
The entire universe is my home.

Sankaracharya,
Annapoornemeshwari Stotran, 11-12

April in Paris

Potage Choux au Gratin
Tofu Quiche
Pommes de Terre Roti au Romarin
Petits Pois à la Français
Prune Mousse

Serves 4-6

Any lunch shared with family and friends can be a joyous occasion. This simple, yet elegant menu sparkles with the rejuvenating lightness of a Paris spring.

Top left – Potage Choux au Gratin: a sattvic variation on the traditional onion soup theme.

Centre left – The Tofu Quiche: another one of Nigel Walker's delightful recipes. Nigel (aka Nagaraj) is a trained Cordon Bleu chef, former staff member of the Sivananda Yoga Centres, and a leading macrobiotic chef and cooking teacher in the UK. The quiche can be made slightly ahead and served warm or cool.

Bottom left – Pommes de Terre Roti au Romarin: roast potatoes take on an invigorating novelty when accentuated by fresh rosemary.

Centre right – Petits Pois à la Français: brings the vibrancy of spring green to the meal, especially lovely if contrasted with the warm orange of Spiced Spring Carrots (page 84). For a real feast for the eyes as well as the palate, add a salad of radicchio and watercress, with French Dressing (page 118).

Bottom right – Prune Mousse: this creamy, simple dessert was an instant favourite when the recipe emigrated to London from the Sivananda Yoga Centre in Paris.

Potage Choux au Gratin

25-50g (1-2oz) butter or margarine
1 white cabbage, coarsely shredded
1.5 litres (2¾ pints) water
3 bay leaves

125ml (4fl oz) tamari
1 french bread (wholewheat, if possible)
300g (10oz) vegetarian cheese, grated

1 Heat the butter or margarine in a pan and sauté the cabbage over a medium heat for about 15 minutes, until soft and translucent, stirring occasionally.

2 Bring the water to the boil, add the sautéed cabbage and bay leaves, cover and simmer for about 30 minutes. Add the tamari and simmer for another 10 minutes. Meanwhile, preheat the oven to 190°C/375°F/Gas mark 5.

3 Slice the french bread into 5cm (2in) pieces and place them on an oiled baking sheet. Sprinkle the grated cheese on top and bake in the oven for about 20 minutes. Serve the soup hot in individual bowls, topped with one or two slices of toasted bread.

• For a vegan version: omit the grated cheese. Combine 1 teaspoon dried mixed herbs with 15-25g (½-1oz) margarine and spread this on the french bread before toasting it in the oven for 10-20 minutes.

Tofu Quiche

Pastry:
200g (7oz) wholewheat flour
50ml (2fl oz) corn oil
1 tablespoon sesame seeds
about 6 tablespoons chilled sparkling mineral
    water
Filling:
2 tablespoons oil
350g (12oz) thinly sliced seasonal vegetables

100g (4oz) courgettes, thinly sliced
285g (9½oz) firm tofu
200ml (7fl oz) water
2 tablespoons tamari
1-2 tablespoons nutritional yeast flakes or grated
    vegan cheese (optional)
pepper to taste
1 red pepper, sliced into rings, cored and seeded
parsley sprigs, to garnish

1 Prepare the pastry first. For the best results, make sure all the ingredients are cold. Lightly combine the flour and corn oil, then stir in the sesame seeds. Add enough sparkling water to make a soft dough, but avoid overmixing. Allow to rest (preferably in the refrigerator) for at least 30 minutes. Meanwhile, preheat the oven to 200°C/400°F/Gas mark 6.

2 To make the filling, heat the oil in a frying pan and sauté the seasonal vegetables for about 5 minutes; set aside. Roll out the dough on a lightly floured surface and use to line a 23cm (9in) flan tin. Arrange the sliced courgettes on the pastry and the sautéed vegetables on top.

3 Put the tofu, water, tamari, and yeast flakes or cheese, if using, in a food processor or blender and blend until smooth. Season with pepper. Pour the mixture over the vegetables and arrange the red pepper slices on top. Bake in the oven for 40 minutes. Serve hot or cold, garnished with sprigs of parsley.

Pommes de Terre Roti au Romarin

6-8 potatoes, with skins on
2-3 tablespoons olive oil

salt and pepper
2-3 tablespoons crumbled fresh rosemary

1 Preheat the oven to 200°C/400°F/Gas mark 6. Scrub the potatoes and slice them thinly. Brush with the oil and place in a roasting pan. Season with salt and pepper and sprinkle the crumbled rosemary over the top.

2 Bake the potatoes in the oven for 1 hour 20 minutes, turning the slices occasionally.

Petits Pois à la Français

450g (1lb) shelled peas
15g (½oz) butter or margarine, plus extra
   if required

2 or 3 large lettuce leaves
salt and pepper to taste

1 Place the peas and butter or margarine in a pan. Gently wash the lettuce leaves, taking care to keep them whole. Do not dry them, but gently place them over the peas in the pan with water still clinging to the leaves.

2 Cover the pan and cook over a low heat for about 10 minutes, until the peas are tender. Season with salt and pepper and add more butter, if desired.

Prune Mousse

250g (9oz) dried prunes, pitted
250ml (8fl oz) water
1 tablespoon agar agar flakes
1 tablespoon honey or date syrup (optional)

500ml (18fl oz) creamy yoghurt
1 teaspoon lemon juice
25g (1oz) chopped nuts, to decorate

1 Put the prunes and water in a pan, bring to the boil and simmer for about 20 minutes, until soft. Transfer to a food processor or blender and blend until smooth.

2 Return the prune purée to the pan, stir in the agar agar flakes and cook for 2 minutes. Allow to cool slightly.

3 When lukewarm, fold in the honey or date syrup, yoghurt and lemon juice. Pour into individual dishes and chill until set. Decorate with chopped nuts before serving.

• Vegans can substitute Toasted Nut Dream (page 115) for the yoghurt.
• Dates or any other dried fruit(s) may be used instead or some, or all, of the prunes.

Picnic in the Sun

Chilled Cucumber Soup
Tofu Veggie Kebabs
Cold Sesame Noodles
Salads
Fruit Brochettes
Papaya Zing

Serves 4-6

Whether in Australia, the Bahamas or California, beaches are places of increased concentration of prana – perfect for meditation, asanas and pranayama, followed by a sattvic feast with friends.

Top left – Chilled Cucumber Soup: sets the tone for our international picnic.

Centre left – Tofu Veggie Kebabs: these can be marinated the day before and barbecued at a nearby lake or sea side, or bake them in the oven and enjoy in your own garden.

Bottom left – Cold Sesame Noodles: these are both smooth and crunchy, a traditional Chinese appetizer.

Not pictured – Salads: Coleslaw (page 98) and Potato Salad (page 99) are the perennial picnic favourites, but all salads taste special when eaten outdoors.

Centre right – Fruit Brochettes: very simple to make and any fruits will do.

Bottom right – Papaya Zing: a delicious, refreshing drink to serve as a start or finish to the picnic meal. Papaya, or pawpaw as it is known in the Bahamas, has a sweet-and-slightly-bitter taste and provides a wonderful source of digestive enzymes. Its effect on both the mind and the body is calming and grounding.

Chilled Cucumber Soup

750ml (1¼ pints) natural yoghurt
½ teaspoon salt
2 tablespoons oil
1 cucumber, peeled and finely chopped
1-2 tablespoons lemon juice

½ teaspoon pepper
250ml (8fl oz) iced water
100g (4oz) chopped walnuts
fresh parsley leaves, to garnish

Combine the yoghurt, salt and oil, stirring until smooth. Add the cucumber, lemon juice, pepper and iced water. Chill until ready to serve, or add 125ml (4fl oz) chopped ice and serve immediately. Serve topped with a sprinkling of chopped walnuts and garnished with parsley.

Tofu Veggie Kebabs

Tofu cubes:
300g (10oz) firm tofu (pressed for 30 minutes
   to remove excess moisture)
1 tablespoon olive oil
1 tablespoon tomato purée
½ teaspoon turmeric
salt and pepper to taste
Aubergine balls:
25g (1oz) margarine
2 sticks of celery, very finely chopped
1 large aubergine, finely diced

1 teaspoon tomato purée
½ teaspoon ground cumin
100g (4oz) pumpkin seeds, roasted and finely
   chopped
60g (2½oz) wholewheat breadcrumbs
To finish:
1 green or red pepper (or half of each),
   cut into bite-sized pieces
20-24 cherry tomatoes
oil for brushing

1 Cut the tofu into bite-sized cubes and place in a dish. Combine the olive oil, tomato purée, turmeric and salt and pepper to make a marinade. Pour it over the tofu and leave to marinate for about 12 hours.

2 About 1 hour before you want to eat, light the barbecue or preheat the oven to 180°C/350°F/ Gas mark 4.

3 To make the aubergine balls, heat the margarine in a pan and sauté the celery over a medium heat until soft. Add the aubergine and cook to a pulp. Stir in the tomato purée, cumin, pumpkin seeds and breadcrumbs. Season to taste with salt and pepper. Form the aubergine mixture into bite-sized balls.

4 Thread the ingredients on to 8-12 barbecue skewers, alternating tofu cubes and aubergine balls with pieces of green or red pepper and cherry tomatoes.

5 Brush the vegetables with a little oil and cook them on the barbecue, or in the oven, for about 15-20 minutes, turning the kebabs once or twice during cooking.

Cold Sesame Noodles

350g (12oz) wholewheat, spinach or
  buckwheat noodles
1½ tablespoons finely grated fresh root ginger
1½ tablespoons finely grated turnip
1 tablespoon tahini
1½ tablespoons toasted sesame oil
1½ tablespoons chunky peanut butter (optional)

3 tablespoons tamari
4-5 tablespoons water
½-1 teaspoon mustard powder
1½ tablespoons lemon juice
3 tablespoons maple syrup
¼ red or green pepper, cored, seeded and cut into
  slivers, to garnish (optional)

1 Cook the noodles in boiling water until tender but still firm. Drain thoroughly and rinse with cold water, then chill in the refrigerator for at least 1 hour.

2 Put all the other ingredients in a bowl and mix together with a whisk. Leave to stand for a few minutes. Pour the mixture over the noodles and toss well just before serving. Garnish with slivers of pepper if you want to add a bit of colour.

Fruit Brochettes

1 tablespoon maple syrup or date syrup
1 teaspoon grated lemon rind
2 teaspoons lemon juice
pinch of freshly grated nutmeg

600-700g (1¼-1½lb) assorted fruits, in large pieces
  (cubed pineapple, quartered nectarines or
  peaches, halved apricots, quartered plums,
  cubed apples and pears, whole strawberries)
Toasted Nut Dream (page 115) or yoghurt, to serve
  (optional)

1 Light the barbecue and let it get very hot or preheat the oven to 230°C/450°F/Gas mark 8.

2 Combine the maple or date syrup, lemon rind, lemon juice and nutmeg in a bowl; set aside. Thread the cubes of fruit on to barbecue skewers, using two skewers per kebab, and brush with the syrup mixture.

3 Place on the hot grill for 2 minutes, turning over after 1 minute and brushing with any remaining syrup. If cooking in the oven, place on a baking sheet and cook for the same time. If you like, serve with toasted nut dream or yoghurt.

Papaya Zing

450g (1lb) ripe papaya, peeled, seeded and cut
  into chunks (retain about 1 tablespoon of the
  seeds for decoration)
2 teaspoons fresh lime or lemon juice
pinch of ground allspice

175ml (6fl oz) fresh orange juice
2 teaspoons honey (optional)
250ml (8fl oz) buttermilk or soya milk
lime or lemon slices, to decorate

1 Put all the ingredients, except the decoration, in a food processor or blender and blend until smooth. Chill in the refrigerator.

2 To serve, pour into individual glasses and decorate with slices of lime or lemon and a few of the delicious, peppery papaya seeds.

South Indian Bandhara

Plain basmati rice
Sambar
Aviyal
Poduthuval
Pineapple Pachadi
Pappadams
Lemon pickle
Natural yoghurt
Paysam
Banana

Serves 4

There is no greater blessing than to be able to give food. This South Indian feast is one that might accompany a birthday party or other 'festive' day when we want to share something special with family, friends and guests.

The main meal is eaten mid-day and rice is the mainstay. Sambar (pictured bottom left) is poured directly on top of the rice. This delicious high protein dish has a very liquidy texture and a deliciously earthy, slightly acid taste. Sambar is also served with Dosas or Uppama with Mixed Vegetables (page 28) or a variety of other dishes for a typical South Indian breakfast or light evening supper.

Top left – Poduthuval: deliciously green.

Centre left – Aviyal: Kerala-style mixed vegetables.

Top right – a South Indian feast is traditionally served on a banana leaf. However, if you don't have one available, this menu is delicious any way it is served.

Centre right – Pineapple Pachadi: lightly spiced pineapple and yoghurt.

Bottom right – Paysam: the god Rama is said to have been conceived when his mother was given a divine blessing in the form of this exotic rice pudding. Known as Pongal, it is traditionally made with jaggery (natural raw sugar). As jaggery is difficult to find in the West, we have used date syrup.

Sambar

200g (7oz) red lentils
1.5 litres (2¾ pints) water
2 tablespoons ghee or oil
1 teaspoon black mustard seeds
1 teaspoon turmeric
1 teaspoon grated fresh root ginger
2 green chillies, seeded and finely chopped
4 teaspoons sambar powder or 2 teaspoons ground cumin, 2 teaspoons ground coriander and ½ teaspoon cayenne pepper
25g (1oz) grated fresh coconut

50g (2oz) cauliflower florets
50g (2oz) green beans, cut into 2.5cm (1in) lengths
50g (2oz) aubergine, cubed
50g (2oz) carrots, cut into batons
50g (2oz) green pepper, cored, seeded and chopped
50g (2oz) tomatoes, chopped
2 teaspoons salt
2 tablespoons lemon juice

1 Place the lentils in a large pan with the water and bring to the boil. Half cover and simmer for 20-30 minutes, until the lentils are soft. Set the lentils aside in the water they have been cooked in.

2 Heat the ghee or oil in a frying pan, add the mustard seeds and cook over a high heat until they 'pop'. Add the rest of the spices, then the coconut and cook for 5 minutes, stirring.

3 Add the vegetables and sauté for about 5 minutes. Add to the cooked lentils along with the salt and simmer for 5-10 minutes, until the vegetables are soft. Add the lemon juice, stir well and serve hot.

• Substitute toor dal or pigeon peas for the red lentils.

Aviyal

600g (1¼lb) mixed vegetables (potatoes, plantains, Indian drumsticks, carrots, green peppers), cut into julienne strips
250ml (8fl oz) water
½ teaspoon salt
1 teaspoon tamarind concentrate

25g (1oz) shredded fresh or desiccated coconut
2 green chillies, seeded
½ teaspoon cumin seeds
1 teaspoon coconut oil
3-4 curry leaves, shredded

1 Place the mixed vegetables in a pan with the water and bring to the boil. Cover and simmer for 10 minutes. Remove from the heat, drain off the water and reserve it.

2 Place the salt, tamarind concentrate, shredded coconut, green chillies and cumin seeds in a food processor or blender with the reserved vegetable cooking water. Blend finely, then pour this mixture over the vegetables and stir well to coat them. Cover and cook over a low heat for 10 minutes. Remove from the heat and add the coconut oil and curry leaves. Serve hot (keep covered if not serving immediately). To eat the drumstick julienne, suck the flesh off the skin and discard the skin.

Poduthuval

1 tablespoon oil
½ teaspoon mustard seeds
½ teaspoon urid dal
1 red chilli, broken in half
½ teaspoon turmeric

350-400g (12-14oz) mixed green vegetables
(green beans, Chinese long beans, cabbage, spinach), finely shredded
½ teaspoon salt
4 tablespoons water

1 Heat the oil in a pan, add the mustard seeds, urid dal and chilli and cook over a high heat until the mustard seeds 'pop' and the dal is a golden brown.

2 Add the turmeric, mixed vegetables, salt and water. Cover and cook over a medium heat for 5-6 minutes, until the vegetables are tender. Remove from the heat, discard the chilli halves and keep the pan covered until ready to serve the vegetables.

Pineapple Pachadi

25g (1oz) desiccated coconut
1 green chilli, seeded and chopped
pinch of mustard seeds
½ pineapple, peeled, cored and cut into small chunks

125ml (4fl oz) natural yoghurt
½ teaspoon ghee
½ teaspoon black mustard seeds
1-2 curry leaves, shredded
¼ teaspoon salt

1 Place the coconut, chilli and pinch of mustard seeds in a blender and grind finely. Mix this powder with the pineapple chunks and yoghurt.

2 Heat the ghee in a small frying pan. Add the black mustard seeds and roast them until they 'pop'. Pour the seeds over the pineapple mixture. Stir in the curry leaves and salt.

Paysam

I litre (1¾ pints) milk or soya milk
3 cardamom pods
75g (3oz) basmati rice, rinsed

2 tablespoons cashew nut pieces
3 tablespoons raisins
125ml (4fl oz) date syrup or honey

1 Bring the milk almost to the boil in a pan, reduce the heat to low and simmer it for about 15-20 minutes, stirring frequently.

2 Remove the seeds from the cardamom pods, discarding the husks. Crush the seeds slightly and add to the milk. Add the rice, cashew nuts and raisins. Cover the pan and continue to cook over a low heat for about 20-30 minutes, until the rice is soft. Remove from the heat, stir in the date syrup or honey and serve.

• Add a pinch of ground saffron with the rice, if desired. Vermicelli may be used instead of basmati rice.

Middle Eastern Feast

Baba Ganoush with pitta bread
Falafel with Tahini Sauce
Tabbouleh
Cucumber, Dill and Yoghurt Salad
Fragrant Fruit Salad

Serves 4-6

Middle Eastern meals tend to be very salad orientated. These recipes were contributed by the very active Sivananda Yoga Centre in Tel Aviv and our strong Lebanese contingent in Montreal. They may be augmented by a variety of other salads and dishes, such as Mediterranean Salad (page 98).

Top left – Baba Ganoush: a cool aubergine dish with a smoky exotic flavour. It is served with warm pitta bread.

Centre left – Falafel with Tahini Sauce: the perennial favourite sandwich filling of the Middle East. Falafel is lovely served with either tahini or yoghurt sauce.

Bottom left – Tabbouleh: a popular grain salad made with lots of chopped fresh mint and parsley. It is delightful on its own for a light summer supper or combined with other dishes.

Centre right – Cucumber, Dill and Yoghurt Salad: rejuvenates the palate.

Bottom right – Fragrant Fruit Salad: a deliciously refreshing citrus salad of oranges, grapefruit, kumquats and dates, delicately flavoured with orange flower water.

Baba Ganoush

1 large aubergine
2 tablespoons tahini
2 tablespoons olive oil
juice of 1 lemon
salt and pepper to taste

paprika
2-3 sprigs of mint or parsley,
  coarsely chopped
pitta bread, to serve (optional)

1 Preheat the oven to 190°C/375°F/Gas mark 5. Prick the aubergine to prevent the skin bursting, then place it in an ovenproof dish and bake in the oven for 45-60 minutes, or until the flesh inside is very soft.

2 Allow the aubergine to cool, then peel it. Mash the flesh, leaving it in a sieve for a few minutes to drain off the excess juice. When drained, transfer it to a bowl. Beat the tahini, olive oil and lemon juice together and stir it into the aubergine purée, mixing thoroughly. Season with salt and pepper.

3 Sprinkle a little paprika over the top and garnish with chopped mint or parsley. If serving as a dip, serve with pitta bread.

• Omit the tahini and use double the quantity of olive oil (or vice versa).
• Use a different vegetable as a base, such as butternut squash, but this is not traditionally Middle Eastern.

Falafel with Tahini Sauce

225g (8oz) dried chick peas, soaked
225g (8oz) dried broad beans, soaked
8 tablespoons finely chopped fresh parsley
8 tablespoons finely chopped fresh coriander
8 tablespoons finely chopped fresh mint
½ teaspoon pepper
1 teaspoon allspice
1 teaspoon salt
1 teaspoon baking powder
oil for frying

Tahini sauce:
250ml (8fl oz) tahini
250ml (8fl oz) water
juice of 1 lemon
1 teaspoon salt
To serve and garnish:
shredded lettuce
chopped tomatoes and cucumber
lemon wedges
coriander sprigs

1 To make the falafel, drain the chick peas and beans. Put them in a food processor with the herbs, pepper, allspice and salt and blend until they are the consistency of fine bulgar wheat. Add the baking powder and leave to rest for at least 1 hour.

2 Meanwhile, to make the sauce, combine all the ingredients in a bowl.

3 Heat the oil in a frying pan. Form small balls of chick pea mixture and flatten them slightly between the palms of the hands. Fry them, in batches, in the hot oil for 3 minutes, or until golden brown. Drain on paper towels.

4 Serve the falafel with shredded lettuce, chopped tomatoes and cucumber, garnished with lemon wedges and coriander sprigs, and accompanied by the tahini sauce.

Tabbouleh

150g (5oz) bulgar wheat
125ml (4fl oz) boiling water
100g (4oz) fresh parsley, finely chopped
100g (4oz) fresh mint, finely chopped
juice of 2 lemons

150ml (5fl oz) olive oil
sea salt and pepper to taste
1 teaspoon ground cinnamon
lettuce leaves, to serve
lemon wedges, to garnish

1 Place the bulgar wheat in a large mixing bowl and pour the boiling water over it. Cover tightly and leave for 30-40 minutes, until the water is absorbed and the grain is soft and fluffy.

2 Mix in all the remaining ingredients, except the lettuce leaves and lemon wedges. Serve the salad on a bed of lettuce leaves, garnished with lemon wedges.

• Omit the cinnamon and add a peeled and finely chopped cucumber.

Cucumber, Dill and Yoghurt Salad

1 teaspoon cumin seeds
2 tablespoons lemon juice
1 tablespoon fresh dill or 1 teaspoon dried
  dill weed
500ml (18fl oz) natural yoghurt

pinch of cayenne pepper
½ teaspoon salt
300g (10oz) cucumber, peeled and thinly sliced
2 potatoes, cooked and diced (optional)
fresh mint leaves, to garnish

1 Roast the cumin seeds in a hot dry frying pan over a high heat until the aroma starts to appear. Remove from the heat and crush the seeds slightly with a rolling pin.

2 Mix the seeds with the lemon juice, dill, yoghurt, cayenne and salt in a large bowl. Stir in the cucumber slices and diced potatoes, if using. Serve garnished with mint leaves.

• **Yoghurt Sauce:** Omit the cooked potatoes and the cucumber.
• **Cucumber Raita:** Omit the mint and dill and add 1 bunch of coriander leaves. Serve with Indian meals.

Fragrant Fruit Salad

2 oranges
½ teaspoon orange flower water
1-2 tablespoons honey or date syrup (optional)
1 pink grapefruit

8 kumquats, halved, or 16 cherries
100g (4oz) fresh dates or figs, halved and cut
  lengthwise
pomegranate seeds

1 Squeeze the juice from one orange and combine it with the orange flower water, and honey or date syrup, if using, to make a syrup. Remove all skin and pith from the other orange and the grapefruit, dividing them into segments.

2 Arrange the fruits in a bowl and pour the syrup over them. Sprinkle with pomegranate seeds and chill before serving.

• If fresh figs or dates are unavailable, use dried, pre-soaked in cold water for 30 minutes.

Winter Festival

Celeriac and Cashew Soup
Green salad with Seeded Yoghurt Dressing
Chestnut Roast with Rich Brown Gravy and
Cranberry Sauce
Steamed Brussels sprouts and/or broccoli
Sweet Potato with Pineapple
Carrot and Parsnip Julienne
Plum Pudding
Holiday Punch
Rich Tofu Fruit Cake

Serves 6-8

Throughout the world there are times of particular joy. The Sivananda Yoga Center in New York has perfected the vegetarian adaptations of the traditional Thanksgiving and Christmas meal at their annual feasts.

Top left – Celeriac and Cashew Soup (page 39) is followed by a green salad topped with Seeded Yoghurt Dressing (pictured on page 121).

Centre left – Chestnut Roast with its chunky rich texture is a vegan's delight. Here it is shown with Cranberry Sauce (page 125). It is also served with Rich Brown Gravy (page 122).

Bottom left – Sweet Potato with Pineapple: not a dessert, but a traditional part of American Thanksgiving dinner, pictured here with Carrot and Parsnip Julienne. Steamed Brussels sprouts and/or broccoli (not pictured) are also served.

Centre right – Plum Pudding: a zesty, healthy version of the traditional recipe, much richer in fruit and nuts than anything you can buy.

Bottom right – Holiday Punch: a deliciously warming drink to serve before the meal as a toast – or later with Rich Tofu Fruit Cake (page 114).

Chestnut Roast

450g (1lb) fresh chestnuts
300g (10oz) mixed nuts (unsalted almonds
    and brazil nuts are best)
200g (7oz) millet
650ml (22fl oz) water
2 tablespoons oil
2 carrots, grated
½ a cabbage, finely sliced
2 sticks of celery, chopped
250g (9oz) broccoli, the top broken into florets
    and the stalks chopped

3 tablespoons tomato purée
2 tablespoons tamari
¼ teaspoon pepper
1 tablespoon dried mixed herbs
flaked almonds, pumpkin seeds and parsley
    sprigs, to garnish
Rich Brown Gravy (page 122) and Cranberry Sauce
    (page 125), to serve

1 Preheat the oven to 190°C/375°F/Gas mark 5. To peel the chestnuts, make a small slit in the pointed end. Place them in a pan, cover with boiling water and leave for 5 minutes. Remove them from the water, one at a time, and peel off the thick outer skin and thin inner skin while warm. Cook the peeled chestnuts in boiling water for about 30 minutes, until soft then set aside, reserving the water for stock.

2 Meanwhile, spread out the mixed nuts on a baking sheet and roast in the oven for about 10 minutes, until lightly browned, stirring from time to time. Coarsely chop the nuts and set aside. Cook the millet in the water (page 46) and set aside.

3 Heat the oil in a pan and add the carrots, cabbage and celery. Cover and cook over a medium heat for a few minutes, then add the broccoli and cook for 1-2 minutes. Add the tomato purée, tamari, pepper, mixed herbs, chestnuts, mixed nuts and cooked millet. Stir in enough reserved stock to bind everything together.

4 Transfer the mixture to a greased 900g (2lb) loaf tin and bake in the oven for about 45 minutes. Garnish with flaked almonds, pumpkin seeds and parsley sprigs and serve with gravy and cranberry sauce.

Sweet Potato with Pineapple

5 large sweet potatoes, total weight about
    1.4kg (3¼lb)
25g (1oz) butter or margarine
1 very ripe fresh pineapple, about 1kg (2¼lb)

150ml (5fl oz) orange juice
1 teaspoon ground cardamom
½ teaspoon salt

1 Preheat the oven to 190°C/375°F/Gas mark 5. Scrub the sweet potatoes and bake them for 1-1½ hours, until soft. These may be put in the oven while it is hot for the chestnut roast.

2 Remove the sweet potatoes from the oven and reduce the temperature to 140°C/275°F/ Gas mark 1. Leave the potatoes until cool enough to handle, then peel and mash them with the butter or margarine. Peel and core the pineapple, using a sharp knife. Cut into small pieces. Combine the mashed potatoes, pineapple and other ingredients. Transfer to a baking dish and bake for about 40 minutes. Serve hot.

Carrot and Parsnip Julienne

450g (1lb) carrots, cut into julienne
450g (1lb) parsnips, cut into julienne
75ml (3fl oz) orange juice
75ml (3fl oz) water
25g (1oz) butter or 2 tablespoons oil
1 tablespoon lemon juice

¼ teaspoon ground ginger
1 teaspoon freshly grated nutmeg
pinch of salt
pepper
2 tablespoons maple syrup
parsley sprigs, to garnish

Place all the ingredients, except the maple syrup and garnish, in a pan; simmer over a low heat for 15 minutes. Leave on a low heat and add the maple syrup, stirring gently until the vegetables are glazed. Serve hot, garnished with parsley.

Plum Pudding

200g (7oz) chopped dates
200g (7oz) raisins
200g (7oz) currants
200g (7oz) sultanas
100g (4oz) prunes, chopped
100g (4oz) mixed peel
225g (8oz) Barbados sugar (or use extra
    dates and barley malt syrup instead)
¼ teaspoon freshly grated nutmeg

½ teaspoon mixed spice
175g (6oz) wholewheat breadcrumbs
50g (2oz) chopped almonds
225g (8oz) vegetable suet
50g (2oz) wholewheat flour
285ml (9½fl oz) orange juice, plus extra
    if necessary
Tofu Whipped Dream or Toasted Nut Dream
    (page 115), to serve (optional)

1 Wash the dried fruit and place it in a large mixing bowl. Stir in all the dry ingredients and then the orange juice. Cover and leave to stand overnight.

2 The next day, stir the mixture – the consistency should be soft and firm, not runny. Add more orange juice if necessary. Press the mixture into a greased 1.2 litre (2 pint) pudding basin. Cover the top with two layers of greaseproof paper or a pudding cloth and secure with kitchen string.

3 Stand the pudding basin in a large pan with 7.5-10cm (3-4in) of boiling water in the bottom. Cover the pan tightly and steam the pudding over a low heat for about 2 hours, checking from time to time and adding more water to prevent it from boiling dry. Turn out and serve with tofu whipped dream or toasted nut dream, if desired.

Holiday Punch

1 litre (1¾ pints) cranberry juice
1 litre (1¾ pints) apple juice
5-6 strips of lemon peel
2.5-5cm (1-2in) piece of fresh root ginger, peeled
    and coarsely chopped
2 large cinnamon sticks, broken into pieces

10-12 whole cloves
500ml (18fl oz) freshly squeezed orange juice
2 crisp eating apples, sliced
2 oranges or satsumas, divided into segments
    or coarsely chopped
honey to taste (optional)

Combine the cranberry and apple juice with the lemon peel and spices in a heavy pan. Bring them almost to the boil, then lower the heat and simmer for 10-15 minutes. Stir in the orange juice and fruit and add a little honey, if desired. Serve immediately.

FASTING

"Verily Yoga is not possible for the
person who eats too much, nor for the
one who does not eat at all, nor for the one
who sleeps too much, nor the person
who is always awake."

Bhagavad Gita, VI. 16

Fasting is one of Nature's greatest healing agents, often restoring health when everything else has failed. It gives a rest to the entire system, giving the body the time to cleanse itself thoroughly, often eliminating impurities that have accumulated for years.

If you constantly overwork the body and mind, without getting proper rest, your system will eventually break down. The digestive system also needs its rest; fasting is a vacation from food.

Fasting is really a rapid curing agent for numerous ailments. It permits the entire digestive system to rest while ridding the body of many toxins. It cleanses the body and makes it much more energetic. Even a one day fast gives a respite. The body feels lighter. During a fast, the bodily energy that is usually directed towards digestion is available for the repair and healing of the body.

"Yogis advocate occasional fasts, especially during sickness, in order to rest the stomach. The recuperative energy may thereby be directed toward the casting out of the toxins and poisonous matter that have been causing trouble. Nature's precaution of fasting to restore health is to be noted even in animals. They stop eating while they are sick, and lie around until they are normal again, when they return to their food."

Swami Vishnu-devananda,
The Complete Illustrated Book of Yoga

"Both fasting and feasting are blessings to human beings. The feast gives you an immediate blessing, which vanishes in a few hours, inducing a craving for more, whereas a fast gives you a different kind of happiness, more lasting than a feast."

Swami Sivananda,
Health and Diet, Science of Yoga, Volume 7

Never confuse fasting with starvation. Fasting is an austerity; it is undertaken voluntarily for a specific purpose, usually to cleanse the system, regain health, or for spiritual clarity. Beautiful for its simplicity, fasting strengthens the mind and the will power. Just as we can strengthen our muscles by giving them progressively more work to do, so we can also strengthen the mind by giving it increasingly difficult tasks to perform. Fasting will help in the development of concentration and mental strength.

Think of the time and energy spent in the preparation and consumption of food. During a fast, this time is available for other pursuits. When the body and mind are not taken over three times a day by the vibration of food, they are left free to focus on spiritual matters. Fasting assists in the attainment of clear insight. All the religions of the world recommend fasting, often with vigil, as a means of strengthening prayer. We are reminded of how Christ went into the desert to fast and pray for 40 days.

Many yogis fast twice a month on 'Ekadasi' days, the eleventh day of each of the lunar fortnights. Considered especially auspicious for the practices of fasting and meditation, the observance of Ekadasi is based on the effects of the Moon on body and mind.

We are aware of the Moon's influence on the tides. As our bodies are 75 per cent water, its effects may be observed in them as well. Without an awareness of this influence, many aspects of our lives seem beyond our control. We are dragged along by the forces of Nature. But a person who understands the effect, and uses it to empower his/her life, may be said to be practising yoga. Even more than the body, the mind is forcefully affected as the Moon waxes and wanes. The influence is so powerful that the Moon is viewed as the presiding deity of the mind.

For the purpose of meditation, there is a great advantage in keeping the body light and the stomach free. This tapas (austerity) helps in gaining control of the mind and strengthening the will power. Fasting is supposed to cause a buoyant feeling. People who cannot observe a total fast may take light foods on Ekadasi days, but avoid grains as they are more difficult to digest than fruit or vegetables.

CAUTION

Although fasting is an excellent remedy, it should not be expected to accomplish the impossible. It cannot cure deficiency diseases that result from insufficient nourishment or congenital defects. Do not fast if you are pregnant, if you suffer from anaemia or diabetes, or if you have had an eating disorder. Consult your doctor if you are in doubt.

How to Fast

A total fast means abstinence from all food, in either liquid or solid form. Water is not a food; it does not stimulate the appetite and it does not need to be digested. It is important to drink plenty of water during a fast as it helps to cleanse the body and flush the toxins out of your system.

When you fast do not entertain thoughts of food. You will not derive the full benefits of fasting if your mind always dwells on food. Fasting is a golden opportunity to turn your thoughts towards God. Entertain sublime, divine thoughts.

Keep yourself busy with peaceful activities during the fast. The practice of asanas and pranayama will help you in the elimination of toxins. You will be surprised to find how much more limber your body becomes when it is not taking in food.

Rest and relax as much as possible. Try to be quiet and to spend time by yourself whenever you can.

Hot peppermint tea is good for helping to banish a headache or nausea when fasting.

Possible Side Effects

• The tongue may feel furry while fasting. Many yogis use tongue cleaners to remove the toxins that exit the body via the tongue. Brushing your teeth or rinsing your mouth frequently also helps.

• Fasting is also an excellent time to learn, and to practise, kriyas. These are yogic cleansing techniques; they are quite easy to do, but are best learned from a teacher.

• Sometimes, especially when you are new to fasting, you may experience some side effects. If you have a headache or nausea, drink some hot peppermint tea. Do not take ordinary tea or coffee.

• The stomach will cease to feel hungry after the third day of the fast. Peristaltic action will slow down and/or stop in the small intestine.

• You may experience some constipation during a fast. The daily use of an enema is recommended during the period of the fast, and for a day or two afterwards, if it is necessary.

• You may feel cold, as the body is not taking in the usual calories (heat units). The process of digestion itself warms the body, as does activity and movement. Many people feel chilled when they are fasting and the body is still. Be careful to keep yourself warm.

• You may feel very sensitive or hyper-emotional, as the fast helps to cleanse the emotional as well as physical impurities. Be aware of this and do not allow swings of emotion to affect you.

Some people prefer to fast on raw vegetable and/or fruit juices, which are a good way of detoxifying the body.

Juice Fast

Some people prefer to fast on raw vegetable juices and/or fruit juices. Although not technically a fast, juicing is an excellent way to detoxify the body, gain will power and strengthen the mind.

There are advantages and disadvantages to juice fasting. Juices insulate you a bit against the stresses and strains of the outside world; they nourish the body and provide stamina. Carrot juice, the most popular for a fast, is an energy drink. It can be drunk alone or mixed with other vegetable juices for a tasty pick-me-up (for example, see Ginger Carrot Juice on page 22). However, one disadvantage is that juices stimulate digestion, so you feel more hungry on a juice fast. Also, as juices speed up detoxification, more people experience headaches and other side effects when doing a juice fast. However, even for the novice, a one-day-a-week juice fast is excellent.

"Raw, freshly made vegetable and fruit juices are very good for those who suffer from chronic ailments. Do not think that raw vegetable juices are like drugs to cure ailments. They are rather the most vital rebuilding and regenerating foods that the body can use for construction. The raw fruits and vegetables are the storehouses of nature's energy to nourish the starved cells of the body. When one intends to fast for a week or two on only freshly made juice, one can drink several pints of juice a day. At times one can feel discomfort from fasting on raw juices, usually because of the stirring up of poisons accumulated in the system, which nature is anxious to eliminate, but energy and vigour return when the toxin is eliminated."

Swami Vishnu-devananda, The Complete Illustrated Book of Yoga

When and How Long to Fast

• If you are new to fasting, it is best to begin with a short fast. If you are under age, discuss with your parents first.

• Fasting on a regular basis helps to keep the body and mind healthy.

• Even beginners may safely fast for 1-3 days without the guidance of an expert. Pick a time when you can be quiet, perhaps at the weekend. You may choose to be on your own, or with a group who are also fasting and will reinforce your resolve.

• One day of fasting each week maintains good health and mental resolve.

• Weekend fasts are recommended several times per year, especially at the times when the seasons are changing.

• Long fasts of a week or more give great spiritual strength. After the third day, you will probably find that your hunger disappears; fast until your normal hunger returns.

A Weekend Fast

Many Sivananda Yoga Centres run Fasting Weekends. We advise students to have a light lunch on Friday and no evening meal. On Saturday and Sunday, they take only water and herb teas. We have an official 'break-fast' on Sunday evening after satsang. This is a communal meal, always enjoyed by all. Most people agree that they have never tasted anything better than the stewed apples served at that meal. They are then advised to follow a regime of re-introducing foods in their diet, and invited back for a 'reunion' meal on Friday, their first day back on a full, hopefully healthy, diet.

When and How to Break the Fast

Many people believe that the correct breaking of the fast is more important, and more difficult, than the actual fast itself. The mind may develop abnormal cravings for foods. Be careful to resist these impulses. It is best to begin eating slowly. Do not take heavy food all of a sudden. Nature takes her own time and course to renovate and invigorate the body.

Eating juicy raw or stewed fresh fruit is a very good way to break the fast.

Day 1: Eat only fresh, peeled fruits, either raw or stewed. Juicy fruits, like apples or grapes, are easy to digest and will help to gently restart the peristaltic action of the digestive system. Do not take starchy fruits, such as bananas, or oily fruits like coconuts. Chew your food very slowly and thoroughly. You will experience an absolute calmness and a feeling of happiness that can never be expressed.

Day 2: Add a meal of raw vegetable salad. This will act as a broom to sweep out the toxins that have accumulated in the intestines.

Day 3: In addition to the fruits and raw vegetables, include lightly steamed vegetables in your diet. Do not add salt or any seasonings to the food.

Day 4: Add grains to your diet.

Day 5: You may return to a fully balanced diet, but try to refrain from returning to unhealthy habits such as coffee, tea, alcohol and meat.

If the fast is not broken properly and the stomach is overloaded by eating too much and too heavy foods, you may get bloated. To get rid of this condition, fast again. Take hot baths and one or more enemas daily. When the swelling disappears, break the fast; this time do it slowly and carefully.

Glossary

Agar agar: also known as agar or kanten. A plant-derived setting agent or 'gel', available in flakes or powder. Agar is available in most health food stores and asian markets.

Ahimsa: the basic yogic principle of non-violence towards, and reverence for, all life.

Ake miso: red miso made from soya beans mixed with barley. Has a rich savoury flavour.

Annamaya kosha: the physical body or 'food' sheath. According to yogic philosophy, each person also has an astral (or subtle) body and a causal body (where the karma is stored).

Arame: a mild-flavoured sea weed (or sea vegetable) that does not need to be cooked before eating. You can soak it in water and use in salads, or add to cooked vegetable or grain dishes for added flavour and nutritional value. Arame is available from health food stores and Asian markets.

Arrowroot: a flavourless, white powdered root used as a thickener in sauces, puddings and custards. High in calcium. Mix arrowroot with a little cold water before adding to hot mixtures. It is available in health food stores, asian markets and many supermarkets.

Asana: yoga physical exercise, whose purpose is to improve control over the mind and promote good health. In Sanskrit, the ancient Indian language, the word means posture or position.

Ashram: a quiet place or monastery where one practises and studies yoga.

Ayurveda: the traditional Indian medical system, based on a principle of focusing on and balancing the subtle energies.

Barley malt syrup: made from sprouted barley grain, it is a natural sweetener with about 80 per cent of the sweetness of honey. It is sold in most health food stores. Other common grain 'malt' sweeteners come from rice and maize.

Besan: chick pea flour; often used to add a nutty, pleasant taste to curries, fritters and sweets.

Bhagavad Gita: the best known of all yogic scriptures.

Carob: chocolate-like powder from the pulp of the dried carob bean. It is rich in natural sugar, calcium and other minerals.

Dal: the Indian term for a dried pulse; also refers to the dish made using the pulse.

Drumsticks: unripe seed pods of a small tree native to India. They resemble long, ridged green beans. Best boiled and then the flesh is sucked or scraped off the fibre.

Dulse: seaweed, exceptionally high in iodine and manganese; traditionally used in soups and as a condiment.

Filo pastry: fine, flaky pastry sold in sheets; used extensively in Eastern European and Middle Eastern cookery.

Ekadasi: the eleventh day of each lunar fortnight. Many yogis consider these to be auspicious days for fasting.

Garam masala: an aromatic blend of spices, to be used in moderation in Indian cooking. Curry powder can be used instead, but the flavour will be different.

Ghee: clarified butter. The butter is heated and the solids removed, leaving only the pure butter oil. Available in Indian stores and some supermarkets.

Gomasio: sesame salt, a condiment high in calcium, iron and vitamin A and B vitamins. Can be used instead of salt for flavouring.

Gunas: the three qualities of Nature: Sattva, Rajas and Tamas. According to yogic philosophy, everything is made up of the gunas in different proportions.

Hatcho: strongly flavoured, dark brown soya bean miso.

Hijiki: black seaweed with a strong taste; excellent source of calcium, iron and iodine.

Jaggery: the dark brown dehydrated juice of the sugar cane, full of minerals. Available in Indian stores.

Karma: the literal translation of this Sanskrit word is 'action', which is understood to also include the reaction.

Kombu: a member of the kelp family of sea-weeds, yellow-brown in colour. It greatly increases the nutritional value of any dish it is added to.

Kome: a variety of white miso made with rice.

Kriyas: yogic cleansing exercises. Many people find it beneficial to practise them while fasting.

Kuzu: powdered tuber also known as kudzo, often used as a thickener in gravies and stews. Is soothing to the digestive system.

Lacto-vegetarians: people who refrain from eating meat, fish and eggs, but do include dairy products in their diet. The yogic diet is a lacto-vegetarian one.

Lecithin: a cell builder, usually extracted from soya beans, which also helps to break down the cholesterol in food. It is a natural binding agent and can be used in baking and in salad dressings.

Mantra: Sanskrit syllables, words or phrases, repeated whilst meditating to bring the person to a higher state of consciousness.

Miso: a cultured paste, usually made from soya beans. High in protein, and a natural source of vitamin B12, miso is tasty and very salty. It may be enriched with grains, such as wheat, barley or rice. It can be diluted with hot water for a quick cup of soup, or used as a flavouring in a variety of dishes. Available as a very thick paste which can be stored in the refrigerator for months. Never boil miso as it destroys the vitamin content.

Molasses: the nutritive part of the sugar cane after the refined white sugar has been removed. It is a good sweetener for baking. Available in all health food stores and most supermarkets. Make sure you buy the unsulphured type. Blackstrap molasses is exceptionally high in iron, and helps to prevent anaemia.

Mugi: red miso made with barley.

Nori: dark-jade coloured seaweed with very high protein content and rich in vitamins A and B1. Nori comes in sheets and can be used as it is, or toasted over a low flame and crumbled into soups, stews, salads or eaten plain.

Om: the OM symbol (see page 8) is the yogic's sacred symbol. The syllable OM is the original mantra, the root of all sounds and letters, and thus of all language and thought. To chant the OM mantra, the sound 'O' is started deep within the body and slowly brought upwards to join the sound 'M' which then resonates through the head.

Pappadams: thin, round wafer-like discs, usually made from lentil or other flours. They are usually fried or roasted over an open fire, and served as a crispy accompaniment to Indian meals. Available from Indian stores and supermarkets.

Prana: the vital energy or life force.

Pranayama: yogic breathing exercises to control the prana.

Prasad: blessed food, usually eaten at the end of each satsang.

Rajas (rajasic): one of the three gunas; this is the quality of over-activity and passion. Rajasic food is avoided on the yogic diet.

Sadhana: spiritual practice.

Sadhus: people whose main focus in life is spiritual practice.

Salted black beans: small black soya beans preserved in salt. Sold in Chinese food stores. The beans have a distinctive taste and are used mainly for seasoning.

Satsang: literal meaning is 'company of the wise', but it is often used to refer to group meditations.

Sattva (sattvic): one of the three gunas, this is the quality of purity and lightness. A yogic diet consists mainly of sattvic foods.

Sivananda: teacher of Swami Vishnu-devananda and inspiration behind the International Sivananda Yoga Vedanta Centres.

Sea salt: derived from the evaporation of seawater, it is high in many minerals, such as calcium, that are lacking in ordinary table salt.

Swami: a person who has taken spiritual vows, much the same as a monk or nun.

Tapas: Sanskrit term for 'austerity' as a means of strengthening the mind. Many yogis fast or put restrictions on their eating habits for the purpose of building up will power.

Tahini: sesame seed paste, high in vitamin E and many minerals. It is very tasty and can be used in a variety of ways. Tahini is available in most health food stores. If you can't find it, peanut butter may be substituted.

Tamari: a form of soy sauce which has been made by a natural rather than a chemical process. It is cultured in much the same way as yoghurt and contains many important minerals, but it is high in salt (though not as high as soy sauce) and should be used in moderation. If unavailable, use soy sauce.

Tamas (tamasic): one of the three gunas; this is the quality of darkness, inertia and laziness. A person following a yogic diet would try to avoid tamasic foods as well as situations and conditions that are tamasic.

Tempeh: a cultured soya food, sometimes with wheat, rice, millet, peanuts or coconut. It is high in vitamin B12. Never eat tempeh raw; it needs thorough cooking.

Tofu: soya bean curd; weight for weight a more effective protein than those from animal sources – and without the cholestrol or high calories. Fresh tofu can be kept refrigerated for up to a week in fresh water which must be changed daily. Tofu is also available in dried form which has a different flavour from fresh. Dried tofu needs to be soaked before using. If you are planning to use tofu in an uncooked dish, steam it first for 2-3 minutes to kill any bacteria.

Vegans: people who eat no animal products, no dairy foods and no honey.

Vegetarian cheese: cheese made with plant rennet rather than animal rennet. Both hard and soft cheeses are available. Cheese made from soya beans, which is suitable for vegans, is also available.

Vishnu-devananda, Swami: founder and guru of the International Sivananda Yoga Vedanta Centres.

Wakame: the most popular seaweed in Japan. It is a fine source of trace minerals and can be used to help soften the tough fibres of other vegetables. Re-hydrated wakame looks like slippery spinach, and is a common ingredient in miso soup. Wakame combines well with noodles, rice, barley and most vegetables.

Yeast flakes: non-leavening 'nutritional' yeast, high in B-vitamins. The flakes have a nutty, cheese-like flavour and can be sprinkled on any number of dishes for added nutritional impact. Available from most health food stores, they are a good substitute for cheese.

Yogi: a person who practises physical and mental control in order to achieve a union of the individual soul with the Absolute.

Further Reading

The Book of Yoga The Sivananda Yoga Centre, Ebury Press
The New Vegetarian Colin Spencer, Gaia Books
The Complete Illustrated Book of Yoga Swami Vishnu-devananda, Crown Publishers
Meditation and Mantras Swami Vishnu-devananda, OM Lotus Publishing
Hatha Yoga Pradipika Swami Vishnu-devananda, OM Lotus Publishing
Yoga Mind & Body The Sivananda Yoga Centre, Dorling Kindersley
The Life and Work of Swami Sivananda Vol 2: Health and Hatha Yoga Divine Life Society
Bliss Divine Swami Sivananda, Divine Life Society